Biblical Foundations in Theology

General Editors

JAMES D. G. DUNN
Professor of Divinity, University of Durham

JAMES P. MACKEY
Thomas Chalmers Professor of Theology,
University of Edinburgh

Jesus and the Ethics of the Kingdom

BIBLICAL FOUNDATIONS IN THEOLOGY

General Editors
James D. G. Dunn   James P. Mackey

New Testament Theology in Dialogue
James D. G. Dunn and James P. Mackey

Jesus and the Ethics of the Kingdom
Bruce Chilton and J. I. H. McDonald

Meaning and Truth in 2 Corinthians
Frances Young and David F. Ford

Biblical Foundations in Theology

General Editors

JAMES D. G. DUNN   JAMES P. MACKEY

JESUS AND THE ETHICS OF THE KINGDOM

Bruce Chilton

and

J. I. H. McDonald

First published in Great Britain 1987
SPCK
Holy Trinity Church
Marylebone Road
London NW1 4DU

British Library Cataloguing in Publication Data

Chilton, Bruce D.
Jesus and the ethics of the Kingdom.—
(Biblical foundations in theology).
1. Kingdom of God—Biblical teaching
I. Title   II. McDonald, James I. H.
III. Series
231.7'2   BT94
ISBN 0-281-04305-1

Printed in Great Britain by
the University Press, Cambridge

FOR ODILE AND JENNY

Contents

Editors' Foreword

The aim of this series is to bridge the gap between biblical scholarship and the larger enterprise of Christian theology. Whatever the theory or theology of the canon itself, Christian theologians have always seen in the Bible their ultimate court of appeal, and exegetes have rightly expected their work to contribute directly to a better theology for each succeeding century.

And yet the gap remains. Theologians from the beginning, the greatest as well as the least, have been guilty of forcing their preferred conclusions upon a biblical text which they could have better understood. And the more professional biblical scholars, too anxious perhaps for immediate theological impact, have often been tempted to produce Old or New Testament theologies which in the event owed too little to the rich variety of their authoritative texts, and too much to prevailing theological fashions. Co-operation between a critical scholar of the texts and a critical commentator on theological fashions was seldom evident, and few individuals have ever been able to combine both of these roles successfully.

Biblical Foundations in Theology attempts to address this problem by inviting authors from the disciplines of Biblical Studies or Systematic Theology to collaborate with a scholar from the other (or a related) discipline, or to have their material reviewed in the course of composition, so that the resultant volumes may take sufficient account of the methods and insights of both areas of enquiry. In this way it is hoped that the series will come to be recognized as a distinctive and constructive contribution to current concerns about how, in the modern world, Christianity is to be lived as well as understood.

JAMES D. G. DUNN
JAMES P. MACKEY

Preface

A happy combination of circumstances brought the authors of the present volume together, in order to assess the meaning – and the continuing significance – of Jesus' preaching of God's Kingdom. An equally happy coincidence, the establishment of the series 'Biblical Foundations in Theology', gave point to their collaborative discussions. Throughout the consultative process which produced this book, the vital interaction of exegesis and theology has inspired us both; our principal hope is that readers will come to value that process as much as we both have. Of course, the dialogue which the series is designed to promote is as yet tentative, and we trust that our contribution will be appreciated in that light.

Although the authors wish to offer this volume as the fruit of their joint consideration, it might be appropriate to acknowledge our respective contributions. B.D.C. wrote the initial drafts of Chapters one and two, and the first half of Chapter five; the translations of primary sources within those sections are his own. J. I. H. McD. drafted Chapters three and four, and the latter half of five. The whole was then written again in the light of comments and discussion. We should particularly like to thank Profs. David Kelsey of Yale and John O'Neill of Edinburgh, for commenting helpfully on various stages of the manuscript, and Dr John C. L. Gibson, also of Edinburgh, for advice on the interpretation of the Kingdom in the Old Testament. Finally, we gladly acknowledge the constructive criticism offered by the editors of the series, Profs. James Mackey and James D. G. Dunn. All of those named have helped us to clarify our meaning and improve its presentation in this volume. For any remaining obscurities or *bêtises*, the authors accept full responsibility.

If there is anything to our thesis, then one might observe that, in the field of ethics, acts mean more than intentions, and that, in the field of eschatology, results matter more than their causes. In a world in desperate need of acts and results, of the transcendent power of God's Kingdom, we hope our little effort will take its place in the struggle that makes for peace. If so, then we will have done no more than the two ladies whom we see, every day, enacting parables of promise.

1

The Kingdom in Word

1 INTRODUCTION

Jesus of Nazareth is probably most famous, among believers and non-believers, as a teacher of morality. His fully justifiable reputation rests primarily on the pre-eminence he gave to the commandment in Leviticus 19.18, 'You shall love your neighbour as yourself.' All three Synoptic Gospels refer or allude to Jesus' citation of these words, each in a distinctive passage (Matthew 22.34–40; Mark 12.28–34; Luke 10.25–37). Paul may have had Jesus' position in mind when he declared authoritatively that the entire law is fulfilled by the same commandment (Gal. 5.14, see Rom. 13.10). Those who handed on Jesus' sayings, then, knew very well that an ethic of love lay at the heart of his teaching.

Even at this early stage, however, caution must be exercised in order to avoid drawing an overly generalized portrait of Jesus as a teacher of human love. Matthew and Mark, which alone impute the citation of Lev. 19.18 to Jesus himself, give priority to the commandment in Deut. 6.4, 5, that Israel should love God first of all, and entirely. The sense of the dual commandment is developed by the distinctive narrative presentations of the two Gospels. In Matthew, a Pharisee, who tests Jesus with the question of which (single) commandment is greatest (22.34–5), is told, 'On these two commandments the whole law depends, and the prophets' (22.40). In Mark, a scribe initiates the discussion, and he not only agrees with Jesus, but observes that such love 'is more than all burnt offerings and sacrifices' (12.32–3). Two factors of immediate interest emerge. First,

Jesus in both passages places the commandment to love one's neighbour in a subsidiary position to the commandment to love God. Second, the significant differences between the two passages suggest that, as the story of the encounter was told, and then written, it underwent a significant degree of interpretation.

Both of these features demand our observation. The first precludes any notion that Jesus was simply a teacher of morality; even in what may seem an utterly humanitarian, or common-sensical, precept, his thought is theological in root and branch. The second feature reminds us that our construal of Jesus' teaching must take account of the interpretative activity of those who passed on his sayings by word of mouth, and in writing. Attention must be paid to the texts of the Gospels in order to assess their meaning, but only critical appraisal can hope to distinguish Jesus' message from its development by those who followed him.

For all the differences between them, Matthew and Mark agree on a central matter, aside from the gist of Jesus' position: Jesus cites Deut. 6.4–5 and Lev. 19.18 in response to a question. In both the Gospels, the inquiry is part of a larger unit in which Jesus engages in hostile disputes (Matt. 21.23—22.46; Mark 11.27—12.40), although the note of hostility is much plainer in Matthew's context than within the passage itself. Such enmity may reflect the experience of Christians after the resurrection; the question concerning the most basic commandment is not obviously antagonistic in Matthew, and turns out to be posi-tively sympathetic in Mark. According to an ancient Judaic tradition, an older contemporary of Jesus, named Hillel, was once asked by a Gentile to be taught the entire Torah while standing on one foot. Hillel is said to have replied, 'What is hateful to you, do not do to your neighbour. That is the whole Torah, while the rest is commentary. Go and learn it' (*Shabbath* 31a, in the Babylonian Talmud). Questions of that sort can be seen as hostile; indeed Shammai, Hillel's competitor, is said in the same passage to have regarded it as such (at least implicitly, since he drove the man away with a measuring rod). But questions can elicit worthwhile rejoinders, whatever motivates them. The comparability of the stories in the Talmud and the Gospels brings out that point, as well as a significant degree of coherence between Jesus and Hillel. Which, if any, of the stories is historically accurate, is a question whose answer is far less evident than the essential comparability of the stories, which makes the vignette in Matthew and Mark appear sensible within the context of Judaism.

The fact remains that in Matthew and Mark, Jesus does not initiate the discussion on love of God and neighbour. He is pressed to name the 'great' (Matt. 22.36) or 'first' (Mark 12.28) commandment, and gives two. Love is not something Jesus preaches as a fresh announcement, but is rather a principle of his teaching which only questioning elicits. That feature of his discourse, common within Matthew and Mark, is even plainer in Luke. There, a lawyer asks Jesus what to do in order to inherit eternal life, and Jesus replies by asking what he reads in the law (10.25–6). At that point the lawyer, *not Jesus*, cites the crucial texts from Deuteronomy and Leviticus (10.27), and Jesus approves (10.28). To be sure, the lawyer's further inquiry, regarding the concept 'neighbour', elicits the parable of the Samaritan's mercy, which is unique to Luke, but Jesus is not portrayed as initiating a discussion of neighbourly love. On any reading, love is not here presented as the programmatic theme of Jesus' ministry.

In this regard, it is notable that Paul does not ascribe his statements about love to the teaching of Jesus. He may assume his readers know enough about the ministry of Jesus to make explicit citation unnecessary, but we could not deduce from Paul's letters alone that Jesus promulgated a distinctive teaching about love. Paul may simply be stating a principle which he believes to be foundational to his gospel about Jesus, and to accord with Jesus' own teaching, without any pretension to cite Jesus' actual words expressly. We can infer from Paul only what we can deduce from Luke, that Jesus agreed to the pre-eminence of the commandment to love one's neighbour.

The programmatic centre of Jesus' ministry was not the concept of love, but that of God's rule. The Synoptic Gospels make it evident that his essential purpose was to promulgate the announcement that God's Kingdom had come near (see Matt. 4.17; Mark 1.15; Luke 4.43). The importance of this theme is such that even reviews of scholarly discussion constitute a literature all their own, and neither the evidence of early Jewish texts nor the principal issues involved in assessing those texts can be explained at all fully here. There is, fortunately, substantial agreement as to the essential meaning of Jesus' teaching, and that needs to be described before our consideration can proceed.

By the first century of the present era, Jews commonly saw God as their 'king', the all-powerful ruler who chose Israel, and would intervene on behalf of Israel. In the Aramaic Targums, paraphrases of the Old Testament in the language of the day, God's 'kingdom' was celebrated when Moses sang of Israel's crossing the reed sea (Exod. 15.18 in Targum Onqelos). More typically, the divine Kingdom was a matter of fervent expectation. The promise of Isa. 24.23b becomes in the Targum:

> The kingdom of the LORD of hosts will be revealed on the mount of Zion.

In the Hebrew text, the promise is that God 'will reign'; in the Targum a fuller phrase, employing a noun, refers to the same, vigorously dynamic and judgemental (see 24.21—25.11) intervention. Use of the noun, 'kingdom' (*mlkwt*), however, is not limited in the Targums to instances in which the Hebrew text speaks of God's 'reigning' (*mlk*). When Isa. 40.9 refers to the joyous, future announcement, 'Behold, your God', it was perfectly natural for the interpreter of the Targum to render the phrase, 'The kingdom of your God is revealed.' Such was the conviction that the future revelation of God's power was to be identified with his 'kingdom', that the term was sometimes introduced by the Aramaic interpreters in an innovative way, even when the Hebrew text they rendered did not require – or even encourage – reference to it.

The Targums by no means evidence the Judaism of Jesus' day directly. Even the Isaiah Targum, whose readings occasionally do reach back as far as the first century, is a composite work which took centuries to develop into the text represented by the extant manuscripts.[1] But critical research has confirmed that God's 'kingdom' in ancient Judaism refers, not to a realm over which God rules, nor to the specific regime over which God rules, but to the anticipated fact of his intervention on behalf of his people. His intervention was considered to be God's definitive, future act, and therefore the end of the world as it presently is. In that sense, the Kingdom anticipated by Jews in the first century was irreducibly eschatological. It is true that the Aramaic term *mlkwt'*, and therefore *basileia* in the Gospels, might better be rendered as 'reign', or 'rule', rather than 'kingdom'. God's *mlkwt'* is his dynamic strength, rather than the area he governs. But 'reign' and 'rule' in ordinary English have an abstract tone about them, while the divine *mlkwt'* or *basileia* refers to God's actual exertion of royal force. For that reason, the traditional term 'kingdom', provided its geographical connotations are not exploited, remains serviceable.

Jesus' use of the eschatological language of God's Kingdom undermines any serious attempt to portray him simply as a teacher of the virtues of love. His stated purpose in the Gospels is to preach the Kingdom, and thereby to win his hearers' repentance in the face of God's imminent action (see, again, Matt. 4.17; Mark 1.15). In a number of cases, Jesus' parables – which largely concern the Kingdom – portray a situation of eschatological crisis, be it as harvest (see Matt. 13.3–9/Mark 4.2–9/Luke 8.5–8; Mark 4.26–9; Matt. 13.24–30, 47–50); as surprising transformation (see Matt. 13.31–2/Mark 4.30–2/ Luke 13.18–19; Matt. 13.33/Luke 13.20–1); as amazing discovery (see Matt. 13.44–5); or as final reckoning (see Matt. 21.33–46/Mark 12.1–12/Luke 20.9–19; Matt. 22.1–14/Luke 14.16–24 and vv. 7–11; Matt. 25.1–13; Matt. 25.14–30/Luke 19.11–27). Not all of the passages just mentioned can be claimed to be authentic, in the sense of deriving directly from Jesus' teaching, but they confirm that those who handed on his sayings understood that eschatology was central to his message. Any attempt to bracket a radical claim in respect of the future from Jesus' preaching, as – for example – a subsidiary element of his Jewish background which he himself dispensed with, is critically untenable.

A consideration of Jesus' sayings in the Synoptic Gospels therefore raises the issue of how his ethical teaching is to be reconciled with his preaching of the Kingdom. In the present chapter, we intend to describe how that issue has been addressed, and why we have been dissatisfied with the answers which have so far been suggested. On that basis, a fresh approach is proposed, an approach which is taken up in Chapter two.

2   ETHICS AND ESCHATOLOGY IN JESUS' TEACHING

Jesus' focus on the temporal transcendence of the world by God's dynamic rule would, perhaps, be more easily understood if his moral teaching did not need to be reckoned with. It is difficult to see, as Rudolf Bultmann remarked,[2] how any one who was convinced that God's definitive intervention was imminent could have spent time arguing about the law and offering advice on daily living. How are these two aspects of Jesus' teaching to be reconciled? As will be seen below, the attempt to eliminate the substantial weight of Jesus' moral teaching has been urged, but Bultmann himself attempted a bold, systematic solution in the opposite direction. As he saw it, Jesus' reference to the Kingdom was, in its own terms, an announcement of eschatological catastrophe.[3] In the face of cosmic dissolution, Jesus issued a call for radical decision in favour of God's own decisive act.[4] Bultmann argued that, although modern perception no longer operates apocalyptically, Jesus' call to decision remains absolute: one can determine to side with God, even if one does not believe in an apocalyptic scenario.[5] Both the eschatological and the ethical teaching bring us before God, in an existentially critical moment in which we either accept or reject his way.[6]

One's appraisal of Bultmann's position will depend on one's appreciation, or otherwise, of his contention that existential decision should be placed at the centre of a systematic understanding of Jesus' teaching. In any case, there is no way in which his vision can be justified or refuted in purely exegetical terms. As Bultmann himself acknowledged,[7] his approach is grounded in the conviction that existential philosophy is the most appropriate perspective for understanding what is human. In the sense that the notion of decision lies at the centre of his system, however, Bultmann gives precedence to dominical ethics, rather than to dominical eschatology.[8] That is, his interpretative scheme, in addition to being overtly philosophical (and to that extent, non-exegetical), reverses the pattern of precedence within the texts of the Gospels themselves. Even among his followers, therefore, Bultmann's hermeneutical synthesis has not won wide support.

Bultmann's attempt to reconcile (or dissolve) the eschatological and ethical aspects of Jesus' teaching may be seen as a response to Albert Schweitzer's.[9] In Schweitzer's opinion, Jesus' eschatology was apocalyptic, and heroically misconceived. Jesus expected the Kingdom to arrive at a definite time, after a period of messianic travail.[10] When he was disappointed by failure,[11] he sought to fill up the cup of appointed suffering by his own, fateful journey to Jerusalem, in an attempt to force God to bring on the Kingdom.[12] The figure who died on the cross was therefore an utter failure, and an offence to religion.[13] If Jesus' intention was such, ethics can only have occupied a subsidiary place in his thinking, as governing the brief interim between the present and the anticipated apocalypse of the Kingdom.[14]

Although Schweitzer's focus on eschatology, built largely on the work of Wilhelm Baldensperger and Johannes Weiss, has been maintained in subsequent investigation, his highly particular account of Jesus' apocalyptic thinking has been rejected.[15] Moreover, his exclusive focus on Jesus' vision of the future does not do justice to the openly expressed grounds of Jesus' ethical statements. The twin commandment, to love God and neighbour, is an imperative without limitation to the present or the future: its claim is absolute. Its foundation appears to be the normative value of the texts from the Hebrew Bible which Jesus cited. They are taken to be immediate and on-going requirements, which do not begin or end with the arrival or passing of any apocalyptic epoch.

Jesus is credited with other formulations of an imperative to love within the Gospels, which make the theological (as distinct from eschatological) basis of his teaching manifest. In Matt. 5.43-8, the command to love one's enemy is grounded in God's impartial mercy as shown in nature (v. 45). We are to be 'perfect', just as our heavenly Father is (v. 48). Luke 6.36 attributes nearly the same statement to Jesus, but Luke's Jesus demands we be 'merciful', rather than 'perfect'. The Lucan wording accords with that of Lev. 22.28 in the relatively late Targum known as Pseudo-Jonathan (albeit with uncertain textual attestation); it is likely that this is the more authentic version of the saying.[16] The citation of a statement which accords with Targumic tradition serves as a reminder that, in his moral teaching, Jesus functioned within terms of reference which were also observed within early Judaism.

Luke's Jesus demands mercy from his hearers as the appropriate response to God's mercy after both calling for love of enemies (6.27–30), and adding what is known as the golden rule by way of warrant for loving enemies (6.31–5). Matthew has Jesus propound the golden rule in a distinctive context (7.12), but both Gospels – perhaps relying on a common tradition of statements (conventionally known as 'Q') – attribute to Jesus a practical formulation of what love means. It means behaving towards others as one would wish to be treated. 'For this', says Matthew's Jesus, 'is the law and the prophets' (7.12c).

Particularly in the Matthean version of the saying, Jesus' assertion is reminiscent of Hillel's principle, that one's neighbour is the standard of love as the essence of Torah (see above, on *Shabbath* 31a). It is worth while observing that Hillel puts the principle in a negative form (compare Tobit 4.15), in that he speaks of not doing to others what one hates.[17] That makes Jesus' formulation appear more aggressive in its demand for love. But such observations should not distract us from the signal phenomenon that Hillel and Jesus, according to those who handed on their teaching, spoke a similar language of love, and that both related love to the fulfilment of Torah. John Dominic Crossan has argued that the negative and positive formulations are expressions of the same basic aphorism,[18] and the Letter of Aristeas 207 should certainly rule out any claim to the effect that Jesus was absolutely unique among Jews in positive stating the same basic principle.[19] It is notable also that the negatively formulated advice in Tobit 4.15, not to do what one hates, is preceded by a positive commandment in 4.13, to love one's brothers.

Even if the Matthean reference to the law and the prophets is put aside as an interpretative addition, the fact remains that Hillel and Jesus placed the concept of neighbour, without eschatological qualification, at the heart of their ethical instruction. Hillel presented such love as the essential requirement of Torah, understood as the articulation of God's will, while Jesus, in adopting a maxim associated with Lev. 22.28 in Jewish tradition, related love more directly, but perhaps just as scripturally, to the nature of God himself. In both cases, what is at issue is God's absolute demand, not the tactics for a particular phase in an apocalyptic calendar.

Schweitzer's peculiar version of Jesus' eschatology, especially when that is taken as the exclusive programme of Jesus, leaves practically no room for dominical sayings which refer to God in himself, without eschatological qualification. Because the ethic of love is accepted as an indispensable, and historically established, aspect of Jesus' message, a revision of Schweitzer's position has seemed necessary. The vast majority of scholars have dispensed with a rigidly apocalyptic understanding of the Kingdom in Jesus' preaching. Instead of viewing the Kingdom as a utopian regime which is to come at a fixed point in time, one might define it as God's decision for salvation, which he has taken, and will effect in the future.[20] Such a formulation admits of both the future emphasis and the present aspect of Jesus' preaching.

When the Kingdom is viewed as a decision for the future which has already been taken, a reconciliation between the eschatological and ethical aspects of Jesus' preaching becomes practicable.[21] There can be little doubt but that Jesus' understanding of the Kingdom was such that it had an immediately ethical impact. The programmatic statements of Matthew (4.17) and of Mark (1.15) present a call to repentance as a direct corollary of the Kingdom: it is not merely imminent, but active enough to require immediate reformation. Perhaps the model of a decision which has been taken, but has not yet been fully implemented, would meet the case.[22] There are instances, however, in which positions attributed to Jesus appear simply unconnected to his promulgation of the Kingdom. Jesus' teaching about marriage and divorce in Matt. 19.3-9/Mark 10.2-12 might be cited as an example of a non-eschatological argument. The appeal to the Hebrew Bible as a reflection of God's nature and will is indeed reminiscent of Jesus' saying about love, but not of any decision for the future; the imagery is rather creational. On the other hand, a recent contribution by E. P. Sanders attempts to interpret even the argument concerning marriage and divorce in a thoroughly eschatological direction. He takes the passage to be Jesus' description of the new age of the Kingdom,[23] which Sanders understands as a regime in a manner reminiscent of Schweitzer's. Sanders is entirely aware of the telling criticism which Schweitzer's position has suffered,[24] and he himself avoids a rigidly apocalyptic interpretation of the Kingdom.[25] But he repeatedly insists that the Kingdom in Jesus' teaching pertains to a social order.[26]

Sanders cautiously links Jesus' teaching about divorce to his construal of the Kingdom as an eschatological regime. The logic of his case is that, since the Kingdom is such a regime, the statement about divorce is probably a mandate for its future order.[27] The difficulty here is not so much Sanders's logic as his initial supposition. The notion that the Kingdom in Jesus' thinking would 'result in a recognizable social order' rests on four sorts of material:[28] the saying about the twelve judging the tribes of Israel (Matt. 19.28/Luke 22.28–30); the question of priority in seating, posed by James and John, or their mother (Matt. 20.20–8; Mark 10.35–45); the promise to Peter (Matt. 16.18–19); and the saying about drinking wine in God's Kingdom (Matt. 26.29/Mark 14.25/Luke 22.18).

The last saying employs an image of feasting, which was used by Jesus in several parables which were mentioned above, and in sayings (see Matt. 8.10–11/Luke 13.28–9) to refer to God's Kingdom in its fulness. But unlike his contemporaries, or near contemporaries, at Qumran,[29] Jesus did not provide anything like a seating plan. Indeed, the point of Jesus' answer to the question about James and John seems to be that people will sit as God wishes, and it is not their business to seek appointed places (see also Luke 14.7–11). In that sense, Jesus seems to be opposed to making the 'social order' of the Kingdom 'recognizable'. His answer is a warning against pressing the image to address questions of status. His antipathy to making an image into a manifesto is also evident in the use of the image of judgement. Similarly, in Matt. 19.28, the promise of twelve thrones is symbolic, in that it is applied to Jesus' followers generally (vv. 28a, 29, 30), not to those specially commissioned by Jesus to preach in his name. The Lucan parallel (Luke 22.28–30) appears even less legislative, since the image of judgement is linked with the by now obviously metaphorical image of feasting. In neither Gospel is a social order legislated by means of the saying. Finally, the Matthean presentation overall does not by any means make the 'keys' of forgiveness Peter's

exclusive possession (see 18.18), nor does the first Gospel relate
the sayings to any organizational plan; the idea that the image
in Chapter sixteen should be taken prescriptively, of an
institutional structure for the future Kingdom, does not seem
plausible.

In all of these instances, more careful exegesis might have led
Sanders not to contradict his assertion that the Kingdom in
Jesus' preaching was not primarily political.[30] Images of feasting, judging, opening and shutting have a necessarily social
aspect, which raises the question of the impact of the Kingdom
on the lives of communities,[31] but to press the sayings for
futuristic legislation is to ignore their deliberately metaphorical
usage. The picture of Jesus as an eschatological legislator is not
confirmed by these sayings, so that it seems unwise to press his
argument about divorce in such a direction. A well authentic-
ated saying of Jesus in fact has it that those who are to be
resurrected do not marry (see Matt. 22.30/Mark 12.25/Luke
20.35–6). Sanders does not cite the passage in his index; closer
consideration of it might well have altered his analysis of the
earlier passage. More generally, Sanders seems not to take
account of the long-standing scholarly agreement that 'kingdom'
in Aramaic refers fundamentally to the dynamic strength of
God's rule, not to the sphere which God dominates.[32] Sanders
is aware that such a view is possible, but he does not observe
that the connotations of kingdom in English (as a regime) are at
most subsidiary within the Aramaic usage, *mlkwt' d'lwh'*. At
this juncture, as well, the option suggested by Sanders seems
exegetically ill-advised.

Many attempts to reconcile Jesus' ethics with his eschatology
rather reveal the magnitude of the distinction between the two.
Some of Jesus' moral teachings are not related positively to his
expectation for the future, and even lose their impact when
viewed from the perspective that the present age is about to
dissolve. Sayings such as Matt. 6.25–34/Luke 12.22–32, where
the problem of anxiety is addressed, do not present the world as
we know it as hastening to an end. Rather, the world appears as
an emblem of God's enduring rule and care for his children.[33]
To that extent, Hans Conzelmann is justified in characteriz-
ing such teaching as 'cosmological', that is, as rooted in the

supposition that the *kosmos* continues to reflect the creative will of God. On the supposition that the world is passing away, the saying enhances, rather than combats, anxious insecurity.

The 'cosmological' element within Jesus' sayings, however, is clearly not sufficiently central to make his eschatology appear derivative; the Kingdom is rather accorded autonomous value within the Synoptic portrayal. Instead of seeking to make one focus subsidiary to the other, the attempt has been made to define a common point of reference which unites the eschatology and the 'cosmology' of Jesus. Christology has been the pivotal concept which has been most frequently proposed. Conzelmann, for example, argues that both of these crucial aspects of Jesus' preaching find their centre of gravity in the indirectly christological claim of Jesus to speak on God's behalf. Jesus saw himself as the sign of God's future Kingdom, but he also took on himself the authority to articulate God's care in the present.[34]

Conzelmann's formulation of Jesus' Christology as implied in his preaching of the Kingdom has a great deal to commend it. To the extent that Targumic traditions were current in the first century, Jews would have thought of the Kingdom as a scripturally warranted promise for the future. By using the Kingdom as his own slogan, Jesus indirectly claimed to speak on behalf of God, and in scriptural language. Yet those who produced the Targums also spoke innovatively of the Kingdom, so that care should be taken in assessing Conzelmann's argument. Of course, the Targumic interpreters did not speak as personally or as insistently of the Kingdom as Jesus did, but they did refer to it without being seen as messianic pretenders. Then, too, rabbis were known to have argued by analogy from God's care in creation to his protection of people.[35] In view of the obvious similarity between Jesus' programme and early Jewish teaching generally, it would seem more accurate to speak of his implied authority at this point, rather than of implied Christology.

For the present purpose, the chief difficulty of a christological solution to our paradox is not that its formulation is exaggerated, but that it fails substantially to reconcile eschatology and ethics. Even if Jesus should be seen as implicitly authoritative in his address on both fronts, we are left with the question: Why two fronts? How is it that the decision to speak eschatologically is related to the insistence on speaking ethically as well? Indeed,

Conzelmann exacerbates the divide between eschatology and ethics by styling some of the ethical sayings as 'cosmological'. The teaching about love, divorce, and not fretting does not express an eschatological perspective, but neither does it explicitly maintain that the world will endure. Rather, the world as we know it is explicitly portrayed as reflecting the enduring will and care of God, whether in Scripture or in nature. At base, these sayings are theological, rather than cosmological.

The extremity of an approach to our question by means of Christology is even more plainly represented by the contribution of Heinz Schürmann. He opposes any formulation of an 'implicit Christology' with the claim that Jesus directly (but without the usage of titles) 'thematized himself *with*' the Kingdom: he alleges that Jesus portrayed himself as the 'absolute mediator' of salvation.[36] The basis of this claim is, much as in Conzelmann's formulation, the evocative fact that Jesus spoke of the Kingdom. As we have seen, early Jewish usage of the 'kingdom' poses a problem to approaches of this kind.[37]

Schürmann's general claim, that Jesus' preaching of the Kingdom was a primary root of his own Christology, has long been a matter of consensus. Well attested sayings such as Matthew 12.28/Luke 11.20 provide more than adequate ground for surmising that Jesus' self-consciousness was related to what he said about the Kingdom. But surmise is a necessary procedure, because Jesus did not reportedly explain the exact relationship between himself and the Kingdom. Indeed, he said remarkably little about himself, when he is judged by the standard of later Christianity. Since that is the case, the appropriate exegesis would move from Jesus' preaching of the Kingdom, which he explained quite fully, to Christology, which he at most intimated by means of such elusive phrases as 'the son of man'. To comprehend Jesus' Christology is practicable, but his self-consciousness is a deduction from, not a datum of, the evidence.

Schürmann proceeds as if the opposite were the case, and the Kingdom could be explained exegetically as a mere aspect of Christology. He accomplishes his aim by asserting that Jesus' preaching of the Kingdom put him on a 'collision course' with 'all tendencies of contemporary Judaism'. In the wake of contributions from such scholars as McNamara, Vermes, Sanders, and Flusser – to name but a few – that is an astonishing remark to make in a work published in 1983.[38] That point aside, Schürmann appears unaware of the evidence, some of which has already been cited, which demonstrates that the Kingdom was a concept current within early Judaism. He writes that to speak of the Kingdom as 'coming' was unusual, although its speedy establishment was besought in one of the principal early Jewish prayers, the Kaddish.[39]

Once he has severed the connection between Jesus and the conventional language of his time, Schürmann can make the Kingdom seem a 'paradoxical, enthusiastic preaching', which appeared to make no sense of the world as it was. The preaching of the Kingdom had to fail, Schürmann writes, just as Jesus himself did.[40] Any programme of exegesis, which presents the preaching of the Kingdom as so cryptic and incredible as to require rejection, must be viewed with scepticism. The Gospels portray Jesus as announcing, teaching, and engaging in controversy over the Kingdom, as if the essential concept were a matter of general agreement. That is precisely what we should expect on the basis of the evidence of early Judaism. Any Christology which destroys the coherence of the Kingdom, which is its foundation, is exegetically unconvincing. Schürmann's contribution demonstrates most clearly that the Kingdom is a pillar in the teaching of Jesus; any attempt to replace it with another conception, however dear it may be to us, will collapse the entire edifice in a rubble of paradoxical confusion.

3 AN EXEGETICAL APPROACH

Recent discussion of the relationship between eschatology and ethics in Jesus' teaching leaves us with our problem unresolved. Even on a revised estimate of Jesus' eschatology, his ethics seem a fresh development. And there is no larger concept, be it ethical, cosmological, or christological, within which the Kingdom may be subsumed exegetically. The eschatological and more properly theological aspects remain.[41] In any exegetical discussion, the Kingdom – not eschatology – must be seen as the leading edge of Jesus' teaching.[42] The very word 'eschatology' conjures up a sense of the other-wordly, and therefore non-ethical, in the minds of scholars and lay people alike. As a result, to think of the Kingdom from an eschatological perspective, and then to apply that understanding to ethical sayings, is bound to generate a degree of discrepancy. Our suggestion is that the Kingdom should be taken on its own terms, and that it may then be explored for immediately ethical implications, rather than run through the sieve of scholarly conceptions of eschatology.

How might this exploration be conducted? One line of inquiry might run through the link between the Kingdom and repentance in Jesus' teaching. We wish to investigate that topic later in the present volume, but for three reasons it must be left unexplored for the moment. First, 'repentance' is a general concept, which fits so well within the theology of early Judaism as to make it unlikely that a distinctively ethical claim could be made by demanding repentance. Second, it has been questioned whether Jesus in fact demanded repentance, despite the evidence of the Gospels.[43] Third, and most fundamentally, no saying attributed to Jesus explains exactly why repentance should be the consequence of the Kingdom. What is needed is a group of sayings which explicate *both* the Kingdom and the appropriate human response to it.

The parables of Jesus precisely meet our requirements. They have long been recognized as belonging to the world of metaphor. In an influential study, John Dominic Crossan has described the particularly metaphorical function of Jesus' parables as that of conveying a fresh possibility to the hearer, otherwise unknown to his world or his language. As such, the parables also invite the hearer to participate in what is conveyed.[44] Both the Kingdom, and the human response to it, are therefore investigated by Crossan from the outset. Crossan recognizes that a parable in the time of Jesus refers to any proverbial or aphoristic saying, especially one which involves figurative language.[45] His further description of parables as metaphors, or verbal symbols, derives from his reading of literary theorists.

Literary theory can provide useful insights into biblical material, if one recognizes that it arms us with categories which are not intrinsic to the documents we study. Within their own time, all of Jesus' figurative devices (of which he was very fond) were parables (*parabolai*, or *mšlm* in Hebrew, *mtln* in Aramaic). But it seems useful, with Crossan, to concentrate on those which are metaphors of the Kingdom; they express most extensively what Jesus wished to convey, and interpretative changes made in the course of transmitting them are less likely to have altered their meaning than those sayings in which precise wording, rather than vivid image, is the instrument of expression. 'Parable' in common usage refers to those metaphors of Jesus which are narrative: stories with a beginning, middle and end. Their function appears to be, as in the case of a father's forgiving treatment of his prodigal son (Luke 15.11–32), to provide us with an account of God's action which is sufficiently close to our experience that we are invited to see him at work in our world.[46] As narrative metaphors, the parables indeed solicit our participation in the Kingdom.

For the present purpose, it may be useful to draw together the notions of metaphor, narrative, and participation. The parables distinguish themselves from Jesus' proverbial or aphoristic sayings (parables in the ancient sense) by their formal structure of narrative metaphor, and by their usage of realistic elements which functionally invite the hearer's participation in what they depict. In both their formal and functional aspects, the parables may be described as instances of performance. The parables are cases in which Jesus spoke in a (for him) elaborate way. There is an element of conscious performance in telling a story to convey a point, rather than simply proclaiming it, or explaining it by means of discourse (which was an option also taken by Jesus). In the case of a narrative metaphor which conveys what escapes ordinary language, only that story – told again and again – can deliver the original speaker's message. The parables were performed by Jesus, and designed to be passed on; the very content of the Gospels, and the history of interpretation, attest how successful his performances were. But the parables are also to be understood as performance in the sense that those who hear them are invited to act on what they hear. What happened to the prodigal is not only Jesus' story; the hearer is invited to consider it his own, and to act accordingly. 'Performance' in this volume refers both to the activity which results in the telling of a parable, and to the activity which may attend the hearing of a parable.

Even the simplest of Jesus' narrative metaphors, commonly known as the parable of the seed growing by itself, manifests performance in both of the aspects mentioned. The passage appears only in Mark (4.26–9), but it is widely agreed to be authentic:

> So the kingdom of God is as a man scatters seed on the earth, and sleeps and wakes, night and day. The seed sprouts and grows, how he does not know. As of itself, the earth produces, first the blade, then the ear, then the full grain in the ear. When the yield appears, however, immediately he puts in the sickle, because the harvest has come.

The movement of the parable, from sowing to harvest, constitutes its narrative structure, despite the lack of any characterization of the parties concerned.

Narrative structure is precisely what generates the parable's metaphorical complexity: the Kingdom is not compared simply to a seed growing by itself, but to a man, seed, and earth (which is what produces 'as of itself'). The parable is not a simple, proverbial saying, nor even does it offer an immediate illustration of the Kingdom. Rather, the Kingdom is conveyed by the narrative interrelation of the tripartite metaphor. The conscious performance of the story intimates the Kingdom it refers to.

The parable is not only designed for performance (as the only means of expressing what it says); it is also pitched to influence the hearer's performance. The final image, of timely action at the harvest, implicitly invites the hearer to expectantly meaningful activity. The narrative from the start has been of a realistic nature. The lack of embellishment enhances the sense that God's Kingdom is accessible: there must be such men, such seeds, such fields, and therefore the harvest may come as the parable suggests. Readiness is not merely part of the narrative world of the parable. Because the parable works within the terms of reference of the hearer's world, readiness is portrayed as an appropriate part of his own performance.

Both aspects of performance, as conscious promulgation and as invitation to action, become clearer the more closely the parable is inspected. The interaction of the various metaphors is particularly indicative of a formally considered performance. The governing metaphor, which relates the Kingdom of God to farming, is a natural usage, given the context in which Jesus

lived. In Isa. 28.23-9, farming is also used to express the thought
that the timely progression of the events involved proceeds from
the counsel of God himself. Within the chapter, the point of the
image is that God's counsel will also prevail in the world of
human events. God's will, as expressed in the natural world,
provides assurance for his people. Within the Isaiah Targum,
that assurance is particularly – and explicitly – linked to God's
vindication of Israel. God's 'kingdom' is not expressly mentioned at this point in the Targum, but there is a close association
in this Targum (as in others) between Israel's triumph and
that act of dynamic intervention which is known as the Kingdom
of God. Consciously or not, Jesus appears to have exploited the
possibilities of contemporary religious language by comparing
the Kingdom to a man sowing seed.

Jesus' parable opens with a concentration on the man who
sows, and a hearer might expect that emphasis to be maintained
throughout. Such is the case in Isa. 28.23-9. But the man is
mentioned, only to be put to one side. After sowing, he 'sleeps
and wakes'; he goes his own way, and seems no longer a part of
the narrative of growth, which proceeds without him. The very
order of events would suggest that the figure who seemed central
is in fact marginal. That impression is confirmed by the end of
v. 27: he does not even know, much less actively foment, the
sprouting and growing of the seed. Now the seed seems to be the
centre of attention, but it, too, is overcome by the dominant
image in v. 28. Just when the narrative of growth proceeds to an
apparent climax, when full development produces grain, neither
the man nor the seed is mentioned. Instead, it is the earth which
produces 'as of itself' (*automatē*). Indeed, the earth is said
literally 'to bear fruit' (*karpophorei*): it has seized the focus of
the parable. By this time, however, the parable has taught us to
be wary. Whatever the appearance might be, the earth does not
produce automatically. The Kingdom is not like just the man,
just the seed, or just the earth, nor is it a haphazard conflation
of the three. The Kingdom is rather like the interactive process
among them which issues in a fruitful result.

When the parable is viewed as a narrative metaphor, a story
performed with an eye to conveying a non-discursive picture, its
succession of images is appreciated. If one looks for a single
point of comparison between the Kingdom and farming, the

succession seems merely paradoxical. But by accepting the parabolic structure, in which metaphor supersedes metaphor (man, seed, earth), one gathers a sense of interactive, fruitful co-operation, and, to that extent, one perceives the Kingdom's revelation. The performance involved in the parable so far seems deliberate, and logically self-contained.

A performance is not only what results in a parable; it is also what elicits a performance from the hearer. Even up to this juncture, the parable, by means of the images selected, has been urging itself on us as a way of regarding our world. If the interactive fruitfulness of man, seed, and earth are 'like' the Kingdom, what aspect of productive, human life is not? The argument of telling the parable would then be that the common life of people is an emblem of the Kingdom. There is, of course, no equation between the Kingdom and farming, but there is an incentive to perceive an analogy between them. And to perceive any substantial comparability between the Kingdom and human living is to imply that our lives have become a field in which the Kingdom might be performed.

The perception of the Kingdom in the ordinary world depicted in the parable invites its performance in the ordinary world in which we live. That invitation does not remain entirely implicit; it is more than a possible reading of the parable's realistic imagery. The climax of v. 28 is no climax; harvest is more than successful growth. 'When the yield appears, immediately he puts in the sickle' (v. 29); the man has returned, but under a new aspect. He is no longer one of the elements necessary for the secret of growth, a secret which remains mysterious throughout. Now, he takes advantage of harvest with a fresh, timely action. Without his opportunistic sickle, there would be a crop, but no harvest. He must act on what he perceives, or his perception – and the growth which preceded it – will be lost forever.

The man appears as involved in the process likened to the Kingdom, and also as its chief beneficiary. The orientation of the parable is definitely towards the climactic harvest, but the Kingdom is likened to the process overall. At any point, God might be seen as intervening, in various mixes of patient action (in the case of the man), germinal growth (in the case of the seed), magnificent fertility (in the case of the earth), and lightning response (in the case of the man's second appearance). But the man who appears at the beginning and end of the parable is not merely a cipher for God. He is also simply a person, someone who benefits without knowing why he benefits. He is called to perform a harvest he did not himself understand.

The image of a people called to enjoy and enact another's harvest was dominant in Jesus' call to discipleship (see Matt. 9.37-8; Luke 10.2; John 4.35-8; and Matt. 20.1-16). It conveyed a sense of urgency and unexpected opportunity. That usage serves to confirm that the parable of the man, the seed, and the earth closes on an invitation actively to perform, not merely to attend. If the Kingdom can truly be performed in the sort of ordinary world portrayed in the parable, it must be perceptible in other fields. The claim of the parable is that the Kingdom is at hand; the challenge of the parable is that the Kingdom can only be perceived when it is performed. Only the harvester, who acts on what he sees, and was himself a part – if only a partially conscious part – of the sowing, can taste the harvest. The harvest is not his, he never grasped fully what led up to it, but he has taken enough part, and remained alert enough, to enjoy the result. The Kingdom in word, a parable performed and repeated, elicits and at the same time reflects the Kingdom in deed.

NOTES

1 For a study of Jesus' relationship to the Targumic tradition which was emerging as he taught, cf. Chilton, *Rabbi* (1984). More technical considerations are available in Chilton, 1982 and 1987.
2 His formulation of the issue has been considered classic within scholarly discussion; see Bultmann (1965), pp. 15-16.
3 At this point in his discussion, Bultmann does not directly face up to the issue posed by Schweitzer, whether error on Jesus' part is an inference which must be drawn on the basis of his eschatological stance and the fact that human history has continued since his time; see Bultmann (1977), pp. 3-8.
4 Bultmann (1977), pp. 8-10.
5 See Bultmann, 1965.
6 See Bultmann (1977), pp. 18-21.
7 See Bultmann (1965), p. 169.
8 For a lucid discussion of this point, see Bald (1979), pp. 38-9.
9 See Bultmann (1977), p. 20.

10 Schweitzer (1922), pp. 359–62.
11 ibid., p. 362.
12 ibid., pp. 385–8.
13 ibid., pp. 389f. It is Schweitzer's point that Jesus' failure in terms of conventional religion is the vindication of his distinctive, unconventional 'spirit'.
14 ibid., p. 364.
15 For an account of research, see Chilton, *Kingdom* (1984), pp. 8–9.
16 For an explanation of this argument, see McNamara (1972), pp. 118–19, 179. Generally speaking, McNamara's book is the most useful introduction to the subject.
17 See Stauffer (1959), pp. 55–60, who argues for a qualitative distinction between the two stances.
18 Crossan (1983), pp. 50–1. Crossan's understanding of 'aphorism', as a unit of communication (rather than an assemblage of words), will concern us in the next chapter.
19 cf. Meecham (1932), pp. 292–7.
20 cf. Helmut Merklein (1978), pp. 142–72. Merklein's book provides a cogent account of the consensus which has replaced Schweitzer's understanding of Jesus' eschatology.
21 In outlining that possibility, Merklein gives renewed effect to the formulation of Joachim Jeremias, who explained Jesus' preaching as an expression of eschatology in the process of realizing itself (1976), p. 230.
22 In a recent article which brilliantly surveys recent contributions to our topic, Hans Bald (1979) has faulted Merklein on two counts. His more fundamental complaint is that Merklein takes Mark 1.15 as the interpretative key for the whole of Jesus' teaching, including his ethical statements (pp. 50–1, cf. Merklein, p. 37). There is weight to his remark, since Jesus' ethical sayings are not strictly ordered, as they can presently be read, within an eschatological context. On the other hand, the essential agreement of the Synoptic Gospels, that Jesus' basic task was the promulgation of the Kingdom, vindicates Merklein's approach. However much we may distinguish between eschatological and more properly theological aspects in Jesus' sayings, the Kingdom is the only systematic category which may be used with exegetical warrant. Bald is helpful in calling attention to the problem of understanding apparently non-eschatological material within an eschatological context, but he confuses the issue by implying that any overarching category other than the Kingdom is provided by the texts. Bald's second objection is more telling. He observes that passages such as Matt. 5.43–8/Luke 6.27–36, which have been cited above, cannot be described adequately as straightforward implications of eschatology (p. 50). Bald stands on firmly exegetical ground at this point, and he demonstrates that even a revised understanding of eschatology does not in itself explain Jesus' moral teaching.
23 Sanders (1985), pp. 230, 256–60.
24 See pp. 124–5, 129–41.

25 See pp. 150–6, 236–7.
26 ibid., pp. 233–7.
27 ibid., p. 259.
28 ibid., pp. 146–8.
29 See Gaster (1976), pp. 441–2, a translation of the Manual of Discipline; and Vermes (1962), pp. 118–21, who refers to 'The Messianic Rule'.
30 Sanders (1985), p. 231.
31 So, rightly, Sanders, pp. 236–7.
32 cf. Gustaf Dalman (1902), p. 94; and Merklein (1978), p. 112; with Sanders (1985), p. 152.
33 cf. Conzelmann (1967), pp. 118–24.
34 ibid., especially pp. 118–19, 147, 159.
35 See the Jerusalem Talmud, Shebi'ith 9.1, a passage given in the name of Simeon ben Yoḥai: 'Not even a bird is caught without the will of heaven. How much less a person.'
36 Schürmann (1983), pp. 43–4.
37 Even more unconvincingly, Schürmann cites Luke 10.23/Matt. 13.16 by way of asserting that Jesus included himself in the foundational preaching of the Kingdom. The passage, of course, refers neither to the Kingdom nor to Jesus. In the Lucan context, the blessing refers first to the Father's revelation to 'infants' (10.21), and then to the dual revelation of the Father and the Son (10.22). The assertion is christologically pregnant, but unrelated to the Kingdom. In the Matthean context, the saying refers simply to knowing 'the mysteries of the kingdom of heaven' (13.11); a directly christological significance is not conveyed by that phrase, nor by what follows it. In neither instance does Schürmann's contention find support.
38 cf. Schürmann, p. 45.
39 Compare Petuchowski (1968), p. 37; and Schürmann (1983), p. 40.
40 Schürmann (1983), pp. 49–50.
41 So Bald (1979), p. 52.
42 Of all the contributors here mentioned, Helmut Merklein has most clearly shown the way forward in this regard. The difficulty in Merklein's study is that he does not explore exegetically how the theme of the Kingdom might have been developed into ethics. Rather, his programme is to surmise Jesus' eschatology from his preaching of the Kingdom, and then to relate that eschatology to ethical material. There is, of course, broad agreement that the Kingdom was an eschatological concept in Jesus' thinking, but to define his eschatology has proved problematic. As a result Merklein does not really move from text to text, but from surmise to text.
43 See Sanders (1985), pp. 108, 110–12, 115.
44 cf. Crossan (1973), pp. 13–15.
45 ibid., pp. 7–8; cf. Jeremias (1976), pp. 20–1.
46 See Sallie McFague TeSelle (1975), pp. 13–17; and George W. Stroup (1984), pp. 83–4. There is a dialectical understanding implicit in such a view of metaphor. In parable, God's action is proximate to our

world, and the parable can also be applied as a description of our world. Whether one starts with the notion of parable as an account of God or as an account of our experience, the aim of a dominical parable is an insight into both at once.

2

The Kingdom in Deed

1 THE SHADOW OF CHRISTOLOGY IN INTERPRETATION

Our reading of the parable of the man, the seed and the earth has opened a possibility for conceiving of the relationship between ethics and future promise in Jesus' teaching. Instead of imagining two distinct forces, eschatological and moral, with a field of critical tension between them, we might rather think of the Kingdom as a single magnet with two poles. At one end is the divine performance of the Kingdom, an inceptive reality which attracts hope. At the other end is human performance, an enacted response which itself elicits action. Hopeful action and enacted hope characterize the parable as a whole, at each point in what is depicted. From moment to moment, as the narrative metaphor unfolds, it may be more the promised harvest or more the purposeful activity (sometimes, inactivity) which is empha-sized, but the parable never concerns merely promise alone or action alone. Indeed, the creative interface between the two is of the essence of the Kingdom which is presented.

Obviously, further reflection on the dialectic here described would be exegetically pointless, unless it could be found to suit Jesus' position as evidenced elsewhere. As it happens, however, just this aspect has long been recognized in research on the parables.[1] In the parables of the treasure in the field and of the pearl, for example, an overwhelming discovery galvanizes the discoverers into unaccustomed action. The joyful news of the Kingdom effects joy in the discoverer, and he acts accord-ingly.[2] In so far as love is the appropriate expression of joy over the Kingdom, parables which portray a loving response might be linked to those of the treasure and the pearl.[3]

The link between promise and activity in the parables, then, appears plain. What has not proved straightforward to interpreters, however, is to explain how that link is forged. Within the present chapter, our aim is to consider several explanations of the phenomenon which have been offered in recent scholarship, and on that basis to develop our own.

Within the treatment of Joachim Jeremias, whose work on the parables is widely regarded as basic, the connection between eschatology and ethics is developed in terms of discipleship.[4] As understood by Jeremias, discipleship is focused primarily on Jesus, so that the Kingdom appears as that which discloses Jesus as the appropriate object of faith. The means by which Jeremias proposes this crucial identification of the Kingdom and Christology demand examination.

Jeremias begins by asserting that parables such as that of new wine (Matt. 9.16–17/Mark 2.21–2/Luke 5.36–9) signify the onset of the new eschatological age.[5] Of course, that parable does not refer to the Kingdom, but is contextually related to the authority of Jesus. Jeremias nonetheless links the inaugurated era of redemption with the appearance of the redeemer in a direct way, and without exegetical discussion.[6] That connection is crucial to an understanding of his book, because Jesus increasingly emerges as the reference of the parables as this pivotal chapter develops; 'realized eschatology' – the notion that the Kingdom has already arrived – functions as the basis of 'realized discipleship'. Jeremias discusses the parable of the father's love, as he rightly designates Luke 15.11–32, within a consideration of the theme of 'God's mercy for sinners'. On the basis of Luke 15.1–2, he characterizes the passage as 'primarily an apologetic parable, in which Jesus vindicates his table companionship with sinners'.[7] By taking an obviously redactional notice as the primary index of the parable's meaning, Jeremias violates his own principle, that the stance of later Christians should not be taken as normative for Jesus' preaching. Instead, he makes the particular, christological interest of Luke into a criterion of Jesus' position.

As his interpretation unfolds, it becomes increasingly plain that Jeremias imports notions of Christology and discipleship into his exegesis of the Kingdom. He styles Mark 4.26–9, which has already been considered, as 'the parable of the patient husbandman', and explains it as Jesus' reply 'to the doubts about his mission'. The complex interaction of metaphors is lost on Jeremias, because his programmatic concern is to explain the parables on the basis of Christology, rather than the reverse. Not even the redactional setting of the parable of the man, the seed and the earth, however, can be appealed to in order to substantiate such an exegesis. 'The great assurance' of which Jeremias speaks in this section relates more to Jesus' mission than to the Kingdom, despite the actual content of the parables which are discussed.[8]

'For he has been manifested whose veiled glory shines through every word and every parable – the Saviour.'[9] The last words of his book are an excellent emblem of Jeremias' programme overall: to depict the preaching of the Kingdom as an occasion for coming to faith in Jesus. There is no point in denying the stirring impact of his formulation, but none either in failing to recognize that Jeremias has, in effect, subordinated the message to the one who preached it. His tendency accords fully with the drift of Christian theology generally; one is reminded, for example, of Origen, who described Jesus as 'the kingdom itself'.[10] Were that tendency acceptable in exegetical terms, we might simply follow the course of Conzelmann and Schürmann, and reduce all of Jesus' preaching, whether eschatological or ethical, to the single issue of Christology. In the end, however, that would be to permit considerations of doctrine to override the exegetical finding that the Kingdom in Jesus' preaching alone had primacy of place.

Jeremias' contribution has occupied our attention in view of its influence on contemporary research. It would not be unfair to say that, since the publication of his volume, systematic studies of the parables have on the whole been derivative. Obviously, research profits when scholars build on the firm foundations their predecessors have built, and much of Jeremias' detailed work, particularly in respect of the Palestinian world-view of certain parables, has stood the test of time and criticism. Unfortunately, Jeremias' predilection for Christology and discipleship has been taken up as if it were an exegetical datum of the texts, and not the contribution of his own conceptual programme. This confusion is compounded when it is presented in works which claim to offer conceptual advances beyond what Jeremias did.

In 1966, Eta Linnemann's *Jesus of the Parables* appeared for the first time in English. Its Foreword acknowledges the influence of Rudolf Bultmann, Ernst Fuchs and Joachim Jeremias, among others,[11] and the book's stance may be regarded as an amalgam of the programmes of those three scholars. From Fuchs, Linnemann derived the notion of 'language event', by which she means that a new possibility for life in the world is offered by a successful parable. Linneman presses the meaning of 'event' beyond the sense of a fresh possibility or offer: she conceives of parables as compelling a decision by the hearer.[12] The focus on decision, of course, is central to the position of Rudolf Bultmann, who believed that assent to the cross was the essence of the New Testament's kerygma. As has already been discussed, Bultmann's existentialism was not exegetically based, so that Linnemann's immediate appropriation of his concept seems hasty. But she develops the notion of decision, not within the context of the cross, but within the context of Jesus' ministry. That reference to the '*Sitz im Leben Jesu*' attests the influence of Jeremias.[13] With Jeremias, she formally eschews the presupposition that belief in Jesus as the Christ grounds the parables, but then proceeds to portray Jesus himself as the point of parabolic teaching.

Linnemann accomplishes her portrayal by accepting Jeremias' finding that the Kingdom in Jesus' preaching is an opportunity for the present. On that basis, she argues that the Kingdom is a challenge to the existence of the hearer which demands a decision; a positive response would mean that one 'now lived by the truth of the word of Jesus'.[14] The last statement cited might have been made as a quotation of Jeremias (cf. above, on Jeremias' treatment of the parable of the return of the unclean spirit), but Linnemann offers it as her own formulation. Once it is made, however, it becomes apparent that for Linnemann what is at issue in the parables is the question of discipleship on a christological basis.[15] Linnemann's panegyric for faith is not, perhaps, as effective as Jeremias', but she of course has every right to offer it. On the other hand, the notions of language event and existential decision make it no more lucid, and they obscure the crucial 'event' in Linnemann's scholarship: once again, the meaning of the Kingdom has been sacrificed to Christology.

Bultmann, Fuchs, Jeremias and Linnemann herself are the scholars most frequently cited in Dan Otto Via's *The Parables*. He also invokes the categories of language event and existential decision, but he distinguishes himself from Linneman. He does so by insisting that the decision called forth by parables can be apprehended without a detailed knowledge of what the hearers presupposed at the original time of hearing. That is to say, in his view the meaning of parables is evinced by the form and content of the parables themselves, not by a hypothetical reconstruction of what people expected to hear, as compared to what they in fact heard.[16]

In making that claim, Via put himself at the forefront of those who have argued that the historical reconstruction of a text should not be confused with the understanding of that text. Once it is found that the parables function to elicit decision, it follows that the purpose of interpretation is to clarify their decisive impact. Via goes so far as to say that 'it is not ultimately the text which is interpreted and clarified, but the interpreter and his situation are illuminated'. He makes that claim on the basis of the 'peculiarly aesthetic function' of the parables, 'which enhances their impact as events'.[17]

By focusing on the autonomous character of parables, Via contrasts his stance with Linnemann's, who in his judgement reduces their meaning arbitrarily to their '*Sitz im Leben Jesu*'.[18] He sees them rather as aesthetic unities whose form and function offer a fresh understanding of existence.[19] At this point, however, Via replaces an historical reference to Jesus with a literary one: he conceives of the Gospels as portraying 'authentic existence' in the case of Jesus' life.[20] Even taken on their own terms, according to Via, the parables reflect the decision for authentic existence which Jesus himself had taken.[21] Not content with making this judgement, Via goes on to say that Jesus' actualization of 'this faith is for the Christian perspective a metaphysical fact'.[22] It is hardly surprising that the book closes with a discussion of the resurrection as a realization of Jesus' 'quality of existence', and as such another 'metaphysical or ontological fact'.[23] By means of a long circuit, we are back to the understanding that a decision for Jesus is more important than his own proclamation of the Kingdom.

2 THE KINGDOM AS THE CENTRE OF INTERPRETATION

A more strictly literary approach to the parables, shorn of such a philosophical programme as Via's, is undertaken by John Dominic Crossan. He developed the notion of metaphor which was taken over and refined in the first chapter. As Crossan points out, it is precisely when the metaphorical nature of the Kingdom is taken seriously that the question of ethics becomes acute. When the parables are regarded as performances of the Kingdom, we are invited to be drawn into that world; but what are we to do in the world in which we now live and act?[24] The question becomes all the more pertinent for Crossan, because he clearly recognizes that action is called for by many parables.[25] Rather than evade the paradox, for example, by invoking a christologically based view of discipleship as the implied meaning of the Kingdom, Crossan prefers to end his book (apart from an epilogue of quotations) by affirming the paradox. Those who accept the word of the Kingdom must be ready for God's eschatological coming, but be aware also that all their readiness is inadequate for the purpose.

Although Crossan articulates the problem lucidly, his welcome of it as paradox is far from a solution to it. The parables of the hidden treasure and the pearl perform the Kingdom as metaphors of action, and seem to invite performance. Crossan's analysis leads more to the passive recognition of paradox than to the enacted response which the parables appear designed to elicit. That aspect of Jeremias' contribution must be confirmed, although his own application of his exegesis has here been questioned. Our own bivalent description of 'performance' deliberately echoes 'language event' and 'decision', but seeks to avoid the christological existentialism with which they have become closely associated. The language of performance also leaves us open, as we should be, to the dynamic challenge of the parables to actual action, rather than mere perception.

Perception and action are mutually implied in the parables of

the treasure and the pearl, as well as in that of the man, the seed
and the earth. Purpose, activity, opportunity and recognition
operate together to reveal what is conveyed. Paradoxical self-
doubt has no place here. Elsewhere, it might be positively
portrayed, but only as a prelude to decisive action (see Luke
16.1–9). The one parable in which soul-searching features as the
substance of plot, that of the rich fool (Luke 12.16–21), depicts
the calculation of advantage as comically disastrous. The
parables taunt the very sort of introspection they might provoke.
They seek action, not doubt.

Because literary approaches have generally employed
language which was first developed to consider modern fiction,
they have stressed the autonomy of the parables, as depictions
of an alternative world. Particularly in the hands of Crossan,
great gains have resulted. It is now possible to speak of a consistent, parabolic focus on the Kingdom, rather than having to
revert to the old convention of reducing the parables to pithy
advertisements for faith in Jesus. But fiction functions to
entertain; the entertainment might be serious, but fiction deliberately fashions its world as an alternative to the one we live
in. The parables take another course. Their realism is such that,
although they do not necessarily describe what once actually
occurred, they operate within the bounds of what might be.

The parables which have already been mentioned evince this
realistic, and therefore challenging, aspect. If the Kingdom can
be presented and perceived as farming, as hidden treasure, and
as choice pearl, where and how – the reader or hearer may ask –
are those metaphors to be realized now? From the outset, the
form of that question is notable. Because the parables convey
the Kingdom as *like* images of actual existence, the notion that
the Kingdom can be enacted entirely within ordinary existence,
as if it were simply a programme of action, does not arise. The
Kingdom is like farming, and therefore it is reasonable to
enquire how our activity *might* be cognate with the Kingdom;
but is is unwarranted to suppose that the Kingdom can be
identified with any activity, however noble it might be. Parabolic
perception leads naturally to parabolic action, that is, to ethics
which are consistent with the Kingdom, not to ethics which are
held fully to express the meaning of the Kingdom. The parabolic
nature of perception and action in the light of the Kingdom

agrees with the eschatological orientation of Jesus' preaching: we speak of, and act upon, what must be spoken and enacted, without pretending that speaking or acting exhausts its meaning. Just as the performance of the Kingdom in word is parabolic, so its performance in deed is not its complete manifestation.

The ethical performance of the Kingdom is not only an appropriate response, it is a necessary one, if the perception of the Kingdom is to be achieved. As conveyed in the parables, the Kingdom cannot be apprehended apart from action. The farmer must be purposeful and wary; the discoverers of the treasure and the pearl must be skilful businessmen; the steward must be shrewd. Without their response, the narrative metaphor could not unfold. Apart from the acknowledgement that human co-operation is involved, one could not even read the parables with understanding. And if one accepts that the Kingdom conveyed in the parables is at hand, that assent involves responding to that which is perceived as the revelation of God's rule. To read the parables is itself an acknowledgement that human action might be implicated in God's Kingdom; to believe them is actually to undertake appropriate action, the parabolic action of the Kingdom, in the present. Because the Kingdom is of a God whose claims are absolute, it necessarily addresses itself to people as a cognitive and an ethical challenge at one and the same time. In other words, people are addressed as creatures, not merely as hearers.

3   THE PERFORMANCE OF PARABLES IN EARLY JUDAISM

The parables are performances, but not entertainments; they challenge, rather than divert. In their quality as performative challenges, however, the parables of Jesus should not be regarded as a unique genre (as they have been presented within some ostensibly literary approaches). The relation between Jesus' parables and parables within rabbinic literature has been evocatively treated by David Flusser.[26] Unlike many of his predecessors in the attempt to describe the Jewishness of Jesus, Flusser deliberately calls attention to the late, post-Christian, date of the bulk of Rabbinic literature.[27] His programme, accordingly, is not to insist at every point that Jesus relied on antecedent traditions. He is rather concerned with the structure of parables, as evidenced within the world of early Judaism, and with how Jesus employed that structure.[28] He repeatedly shows that the distinctiveness of Jesus' parables is appreciated under a comparative approach.[29]

Flusser begins by making a distinction between parables of early Judaism, which he describes as 'classical', and those of Rabbinic Judaism after AD 70, which he describes as 'exegetical'.[30] The latter type of parable is discerned with reference to its midrashic purpose: the parable is alleged to illuminate a biblical passage or passages. Early Jewish parables, even if biblical verses are cited within them, have an ethical, rather than a midrashic, purpose. They function to awaken the hearer to the moral imperative they convey.[31] They are told realistically, but they should be described as pseudo-realistic. Flusser insists on this qualification, in view of the highly stylized character of such parables, but also for a more profound reason. They awaken the hearer to a moral imperative, but one which is only describable by analogy to the parable, not in a discursive statement.[32]

In order to evaluate Flusser's observations, certain of his examples must be cited. They not only establish much of his analysis, but are illuminating in their own right. One of the most notable of early Jewish parables is ascribed to Yoḥanan ben Zakkai, perhaps the most important figure in the reconstruction of Judaism after AD 70.[33] A king invited his servants to a feast, without announcing the hour of the meal. Wise servants attired themselves properly, and waited at the door of the king's house. Foolish servants expected definite signs of the meal's preparation, and went about their work until they should see them. When the king appeared without further ado, the wise enjoyed a fine meal, and the foolish, work-soiled servants were made to stand and watch.

Jesus, of course, never told this parable, but many parables comparable to it are ascribed to him. The motif of a festal banquet, as has already been discussed, is central within Jesus' parables and sayings. Moreover, the particularly royal nature of the banquet is stressed from time to time, especially in the Matthean parable of the wedding feast (22.1–14, cf. Luke 14.16–24). Matthew's reference to a sub-plot concerning the wedding garment (vv. 11-13) provides another point of comparison.[34] It must be stressed, however, that the narrative development of the two parables is quite distinctive. Where Yoḥanan speaks of servants who either are or are not prudential, Jesus speaks of guests invited by servants, and the extraordinarily bad, sometimes violent, behaviour of those invited gives the parable its on-going impetus. As Flusser knows, the parable in its present form should probably not be taken as Jesus' own formulation, and it may even allude to the destruction of Jerusalem by fire in 22.7.[35] The point nonetheless remains that, as the parables of Jesus and Yoḥanan have been handed down (whether or not accurately), they share a fundamental motif and a similar structure.[36] Flusser himself does not refer to this structure as narrative metaphor, but in view of our discussion, such a designation appears appropriate.

Flusser offers a long treatment of another, comparable parable, that of the wise and foolish virgins in Matt. 25.1-13. He refers to the wedding as the 'theme' of the parable, rather than as a motif.[37] But if the term 'theme' is used both to refer to a leading motif, and to the point of the story, confusion becomes all too easy. It seems wise to speak simply of the motifs from which a parable is constructed, and of the themes which emerge as a result of its being told.

There is a thematic similarity among Jesus' two parables of a wedding feast in Matthew, and Yoḥanan's parable of a royal banquet. In all three cases, a readiness to accept, and act upon, an invitation is called for, on the understanding that the king who invites is none other than God. In each parable, however, a particular sort of readiness is urged on the hearer, a readiness defined by the narrative metaphor involved. Yoḥanan's narrative involves dropping normal obligations to await God's promised banquet, while Jesus' parable of recalcitrant guests is more complex. The latter narrative warns against obstinacy, and offers the hope of inclusion in God's promise to those who were not initially invited (22.8-10), provided they are fit to accept the invitation (vv. 11-14). Finally, the parable of the wise and foolish virgins provides a warning of the foresight (25.3-4, 7-12), as well as of the patience (vv. 5-7), which readiness for God's promise involves. The three parables develop their living distinctiveness in the creative tension the hearer experiences between what is happening in the story and what is expected from him. That is, the discernment of ethical theme is as crucial in the understanding of parables as the observation of narrative motif. When the language of theme is employed to discover the imperative aspect of parables, their ethical focus appears more cogent.[38]

Early Jewish parables (Jesus' included) exploit the tension any hearer might experience between the specific demands of the parabolic situation, and the lack of precise guidance in the present. It is as if the king one waits on had departed, which is precisely a motif certain parables take up. Nathan told a parable,[39] in which a king built a palace, brought in servants, and entrusted them with gold and silver. Warning them not to steal, he went to another province. The servants so exploited one another, that the king returned to find his servants standing naked outside the palace. The king took back what was stolen. A similar motif is developed, again distinctively, in the parable of the demanding owner (Matt. 25.14–30; Luke 19.12–27, where the owner is a royal figure, v. 12).[40] The narrative metaphor in the latter case, however, is of productive enterprise, rather than of simple honesty, as the appropriate response to the king's absence. There is also a notable difference between the parables in the conditions under which the king or the owner departs. Nathan's king tells the servants not to do what they proceed to take to surreal lengths. Jesus' owner requires what he did not explicitly command. The ethical themes of the two parables are in quite different keys. In both cases, however, the moment at which the parable becomes surreal is also the moment at which its ethical theme becomes plainest. Just because Nathan's servants are depicted as so ludicrously selfish, the hearer is to avoid any such expropriation. Just because Jesus' owner is so eager for gain, the hearer is to redouble his productivity.

What Flusser calls 'pseudo-realism', and is here designated as 'surrealism', is indeed central to an understanding of the parables. It is obviously a feature in Yohanan's story of an almost whimsical king, as well as in Nathan's story of stupidly selfish servants. Jesus' foolish virgins are no brighter, and the behaviour of those invited to a wedding feast in Matt. 22.1–14 is inexplicably bad. At no point are these heightened motifs out of keeping with the thematic impetus behind what is narrated. Yoḥanan warns that wary readiness is necessary when the divine king issues his unqualified invitation. The wedding feast in Matt. 22.1–14 is, at the same time, an open invitation and a threat to those who fail to accept it.

Even in the parables of growth, where the realism is nearly naturalistic, elements of hyperbole (if not surrealism) are plain. In the narrative of the man, the seed and the earth, action is abrupt and unmotivated. The man sleeps for no apparent reason, and then puts in his sickle 'immediately'; the seed sprouts in no stated time, and the earth just produces 'as of itself'. Similarly, mustard seed becomes a 'tree' (see Matt. 13.31–2/Luke 13.18–19), or makes 'big branches' (Mark 4.30–2) without an interval of time being indicated; the point is beginning and result, rather than process. The hyperbolic comparison of start and finish is also evident in the parable of the leaven (Matt. 13.33/Luke 13.20–1).[41] The parables of the hidden treasure and the pearl (Matt. 13.44–6) are surprising, rather than hyperbolic, where they concern the discovery of what is valuable (vv. 44a, 45, 46a), but the reaction of those who find them, in selling everything to acquire them, is exaggerated (vv. 44b, 46b). In these cases also, ethical themes are especially conveyed by the least realistic motifs. The strange activities of man, seed and earth (Mark 4.26–9) articulate the co-operative revelation of the Kingdom, a revelation whose performance the hearer may perceive in unexpected quarters. And it may be revealed as suddenly as the depiction of what mustard seed and leaven do. When that occurs, radical response, the relinquishment of every other priority, is appropriate, as when the treasure and the pearl were found.[42] As Flusser rightly remarks, the parables of growth are unusual in literary terms, since precise analogies in Rabbinic literature have not been discovered. Agricultural motifs appear incidentally in Rabbinic parables, but not as the leading motif.[43] A claim on this basis to the effect that Jesus was unique, however, would be hasty. The very fact that the early Jewish fashion for parables was later superseded suggests that our information about them is limited, since the bulk of Rabbinica was composed after that period. But on the evidence as it stands, Jesus' parables of growth do appear distinctive.

Flusser compares such parables, especially that of the man, the seed and the earth, with one attributed to Epictetus.[44] Epictetus uses a parable of growth in order to recommend patience (*Diatribes* 1.15.6–8): if it is necessary to wait for a grape or a fig, for bloom, fruit and ripening, how can anyone hope for the sympathy of one's brother in a short time? Flusser acknowledges that the purpose of the imagery of growth in Jesus' parable is quite different from Epictetus', but he does not say *how* it is different.

Aside from the metaphorical complexity of Jesus' parable, its eschatological emphasis distinguishes it from Epictetus'. The narrative co-ordination of Jesus' images leads inexorably to harvest, not merely ripening, as the climax of the process described. When the motifs of a parable of the Kingdom converge on an image of the final disclosure of what has been implicitly developing all along, the emphasis on eschatology seems apparent. That emphasis, in turn, substantially affects the perceived ethical theme of the parable. The ethics of Jesus involve a co-operative response to the Kingdom, in the expectation that its ultimate disclosure is near; Epictetus speaks of human sympathy as if it were analogous to what ordinarily blossoms, ripens (and dies). Even Jesus' usage of natural imagery heralds a hope of transcendence, and calls to action grounded in the hope of that transcendence.[45]

Consideration of Flusser's approach, once the necessary criticisms of its execution are taken into account, enables us to refine the notion of performance in Jesus' parables. The use and co-ordination of motifs constitutes their performance as aesthetic wholes. Their thematic call for action establishes, or at least invites, their performance in ethical terms. But the two levels, aesthetic and ethical, are closely related, and both are irreducibly eschatological. Parabolic motifs indeed portray divine action as inceptive, but not as perfected: the narrative action points towards the future as the locus of the Kingdom's ultimate disclosure. Similarly, the ethical themes of the parables frame and encourage a wary, clever – even opportunistic – response to the disclosure which is under way, but not complete. The ethics involved are not 'interim', in the sense of limited to a temporal dispensation, but neither are they autonomously recommended. They are only appropriate as responses to the

Kingdom's disclosure; they have no standing as absolute imperatives. There is no good and no evil, within Jesus' parabolic world, aside from the revelation of the Kingdom.

4   PARABOLIC ETHICS IN JESUS' TEACHING

The expression of ethics by means of parables is a common element, shared by Jesus and some of his near contemporaries. The leading edge of eschatology, at the levels of motif and theme, gives his parables a certain degree of distinctiveness; their focus on the Kingdom is characteristic of him. Their complexity as narrative metaphor, and their development of motifs of growth, also provide evidence of Jesus' distinctiveness as a teacher of eschatology and ethics, without giving credibility to any portrayal of him as being absolutely unique in historical terms.

Jesus' emphasis on love, once it is seen as the appropriate response to God's revelation in his Kingdom, becomes quite explicable. The parables depict the Kingdom as divine activity by means of motifs of narrative metaphor. Their ethical themes emerge as those motifs engage the hearer as responses to the Kingdom which is depicted. A similar dynamic between motif and theme is evident in teachings which are normally described as ethical. The dynamic is most obvious in the statement that Jesus' hearers are to be 'perfect', or 'merciful', just as their heavenly Father is (Matt. 5.48; Luke 6.36): the nature of God is in itself a programme for humanity. Unless it is understood that what God is has implications for what people should be, the logic of the imperative cannot be grasped. But the dominant portrayal of God in Jesus' teaching is under the category of the Kingdom. It is therefore implicit that what God does, as active rule, is to be accepted by means of a positive response. A loving king, by the very power of his love, requires loving subjects (see also Matt. 18.23–35).[46]

Once the relationship between what God lovingly performs, and the performance he requires, is understood, other ethical imperatives also find their centre of gravity. The instructions of God in Deut. 6.4–5 and Lev. 19.18 are expressions of the divine king, which particularly reflect both his own nature and (for that reason) the way of his Kingdom. That Jesus chose just those passages in framing the most basic commandment (Matt. 22.34-40/Mark 12.28-34; cf. Luke 10.25-9) is therefore consistent with his eschatological thinking. Of course, the focus on love is not merely derivative from eschatology; but, once love is seen as of the very essence of God, the disclosure of his Kingdom makes love an absolute imperative. Even Jesus' teaching about marriage and divorce (Matt. 19.3-9; Mark 10.2-12) appears less out of keeping with his eschatology when it is approached from the present perspective. Just as the parables of growth imply ethical themes, so the understanding that God created male and female for each other is relevant to the question of human partnership: creational 'motifs' imply marital 'themes'.

At no point in interpreting the ethical sayings is there any reason to deny that eschatology might still be in view, and still less to assert that eschatology is contradicted. God's perfection in mercy or love is at least partially reflected in his will ultimately to vindicate his people. The same God who calls those who are apparently unworthy to his final banquet (see Matt. 22.9-10/ Luke 14.21b-23) also makes his sun shine on the just and the unjust (Matt. 5.45). And the God who is metaphorically depicted as eschatologically active in the parables is identical with the one who demands love and marital fidelity. The systematic centre, which unites Jesus' preaching of the Kingdom and his teaching of ethics, is neither Christology, nor an appeal to the wisdom of the established world. Rather, both articulate what it means for God to be commencing his final, powerful reign.

The content of the parables and the ethical instructions are indeed different, and their emphases vary, but they exploit the single dynamic between motif and theme in their distinctive ways. The parables concentrate on developing their motifs of narrative metaphor, and the hearer is left to infer the theme of ethics. In the ethical sayings, on the other hand, the theme is plainly stated, and the underlying conception of God remains to be gathered. The latter aspect has provided some interpreters with an opportunity to read their own conception of God, generally a christological one, into the background of the sayings. That tendency has generated the apparent contradiction between ethics and eschatology in Jesus' position. But the contradiction is eliminated when the Kingdom, as conveyed by narrative metaphor, is seen as providing the theological basis of Jesus' ethics.

In what has been said on the basis of Flusser's investigation, no appeal has been made to the notion of discipleship as developed by Jeremias. That is a natural outcome of comparing Jesus' parables with early Jewish analogies, where such a notion is not apparent. It also permits the Kingdom to stand at the systematic centre of the parables (and of ethics), instead of being dissolved in a Christology of discipleship. The fact remains, however, that Jesus' usage of early Jewish motifs is characterized on occasion by an appeal for discipleship, in the context of his announcement of the Kingdom. It remains to be explained how that appeal is consistent with our understanding of the Kingdom as performance.

A saying of Rabbi Tarfon (who lived around AD 100), compares learning Torah to a day of labour (*Avoth* 2.15–16).[47] The day is short, the work great; the workers are recalcitrant, but the reward immense. The taskmaster presses, but he will pay reliably. Flusser presupposes that, before Tarfon, this parable was not applied to learning Torah, but to human life generally. Jesus, according to Flusser, adapted the motif in order to send out his followers to preach the Kingdom.[48]

Flusser's supposition that Jesus adapted an earlier form of Tarfon's statement is not provable, and is unnecessary in any case. Comparison is possible, without deriving one saying from the other. Flusser rightly points out that Jesus' saying is far more urgent than Tarfon's: the hour of harvest has come, and must be acted upon. That motival and thematic eschatology (which is not so designated by Flusser) is precisely what distinguishes Jesus' statement from Tarfon's. Another distinguishing factor is the use of the saying in order to send out followers to preach. In Matthew, the saying appears immediately before Jesus' commission of twelve 'disciples' (10.1), or 'apostles' (10.2; 9.37–8) to proclaim the Kingdom and heal. In Luke, the saying appears within the similar commission of seventy-two of Jesus' followers (10.1–12; v.2).

In his recent book on Jesus, E. P. Sanders rightly speaks of Jesus' call of disciples as being one of the 'almost indisputable facts' of his ministry.[49] That judgement is richly supported by scholarly consensus, and Sanders proceeds to argue, once again in close agreement with others, that the number twelve suggests that Jesus' task included the restoration of Israel's twelve tribes. The hope that Israel would be restored to full allegiance to God, and to territorial integrity, was axiomatic in early Judaism, and does appear to have been central within Jesus' purpose.[50] A positive response to the Kingdom is what Jesus' followers are sent to achieve, as the condition of Israel's restoration (see Matt. 10.5–15 and Luke 10.3–12).[51]

The urgent need for response is clearly indicated in the commissioning of the twelve, and the seventy-two, and is consistent with sayings attributed to Jesus himself. His opening statement in Mark 1.15 demands repentance and belief in his message as responses to the Kingdom; the Matthean counterpart (4.17) refers only to repentance. Sanders, however, has mounted an attack on the consensus that Jesus called for repentance in view of the Kingdom.[52] He regards the evidence of the passages just cited as 'relatively speaking, slight', by which he means that they may have been subjected to a degree of Christian interpretation.[53] On Sanders' understanding, 'There is a puzzle with regard to Jesus' view of sinners: we do not know just how he expected them to live after their acceptance of his message.'[54] That problem, in our view, is somewhat artificial, in that it is caused by Sanders' rejection of the very evidence that would have solved it.

Sanders builds a great deal on his finding; he argues that Jesus offered the Kingdom to the wicked without repentance.[55] He is well aware that parables such as that of the lost sheep, in Matt. 18.12–24/Luke 15.4–7, concern repentance, 'but apparently individual repentance'.[56] He does not appreciate, it would seem, that the controlling metaphor involves God as a shepherd and Israel as his flock, as is consistent with biblical usage and Jesus' metaphorical habits.[57] Sanders' sharp distinction between individual and communal repentance cannot be maintained. He is correct in saying that 'there is not a significant body of reliable sayings material which *explicitly* attributes to Jesus a call for *national* repentance',[58] but only if the italics in that statement are carefully observed. Even then, it is surely appropriate to bear in mind that Jesus was in no position himself to address Israel generally, as occurs in the published documents of early Judaism: his own words were addressed to particular hearers on specific occasions. When Jesus did approximate to that position, by means of his commissioned disciples, it is notable that they preach 'in order that people might repent' (Mark 6.12). Sanders takes that statement, and those like it, as 'editorial',[59] and it clearly is of a summary nature (whatever its provenance). But to argue on that basis that Jesus did not emphasize repentance is curious in the extreme: the operating assumption would seem to be that Jesus stood for the opposite of everything that is interpretative in the Gospels.

Sanders is well aware of the oddity of his position. He acknowledges that repentance was an aspect of the conventional theology of early Judaism, and that John the Baptist emphasized it.[60] On both counts, one would expect Jesus to have accepted repentance as part of his normal religious vocabulary. Instead, Sanders claims that, 'in view of the eschaton he did not deal with their [sc. his hearers] behaviour, and thus could truly be criticized for including the wicked in his "kingdom"'.[61] Such a judgement can only be reached by programmatically excluding evidence, as we have already seen, and by ignoring the ethical themes of the parables. In the Kingdom they convey, the farmer must be punctual, ready and swift; discoverers of treasure and pearls must be prepared to sell everything to acquire them; potential guests must heed invitations, give up their normal activities, and be properly attired when the hour for feasting arrives. Penitent renunciation is certainly not demanded for its own sake, but it is implicit within a positive response to the Kingdom as supremely valuable: if the Kingdom is worth every-thing, it might come at the price of everything. Repentance, a turning back to what alone has value, is a necessary and inescapable aspect of entering the Kingdom.

The motif of 'entering' the Kingdom, which is so signal within Jesus' sayings, itself illustrates an ethic of penitent response. It is a metaphor sometimes of a seemingly impossible struggle, perhaps more difficult than a camel squeezing through a needle's eye (Matt. 19.24/Mark 10.25/Luke 18.25), or as vexing as becoming children again (Matt. 18.3/Mark 10.15/Luke 18.17; see John 3.3-4). In both cases, the language of the Kingdom is employed to insist that there is a presently realizable way of accepting God. The king rules even now, and obedience to him constitutes entry into his Kingdom, and the rich promises of that Kingdom. But wealth is an obstacle to entry, and even the status of adulthood must be given up in childlike responsiveness.[62] Although the commands to enter the Kingdom are not parables, in the sense which has been discussed here, they involved the use of metaphor in order to convey an ethical theme by means of one or more motifs. For that reason, they also belong within the category of the Kingdom's performance.

To enter the kingdom is said to be 'difficult' (Matt. 19.23; Mark 10.23-4; Luke 18.24), not impossible, for those with wealth. The ethic of renunciation is not so articulated that entry is limited to disciples, who have given up 'everything' (Matt. 19.27; Mark 10.28), or their 'own' (Luke 18.28). The disciples are placed in a position of relative, not absolute, privilege. The statement about becoming a child appears in the general form, 'Whoever does not receive the kingdom as a child will not enter it', in Mark (10.15) and Luke (18.17), and therefore is not exclusively a promise to disciples. In Matthew, the statement is addressed to the disciples (18.3), but is immediately followed by two general teachings of the same type, which refer to people beyond the circle of Jesus' disciples (18.4-5). Clearly, the ethic of the Kingdom cannot be equated simply with discipleship.

The question of entering the Kingdom is not unlike that of understanding the parables, which is as we would expect, if the interface between the Kingdom and ethics (as described here) can be maintained. Here, too, the disciples are put in a position of relative privilege: Jesus explains the parables to them, not to outsiders (see Matt. 13.10-11; Mark 4.11; Luke 8.10). But those from the group of disciples are commissioned to promulgate the message of the Kingdom in public, as we have seen, so that their privilege is not absolute. Discipleship is not the end of the Kingdom, whether it is viewed theologically or ethically; rather, discipleship is the means by which the motifs and ethical themes of the Kingdom are communicated. For that reason, discipleship cannot be equated with the performance of the Kingdom. Disciples are certainly expected to perform it, in the two senses of conveying and enacting the Kingdom, but their function in preaching and healing, like Jesus' function, is to occasion the performance of the Kingdom among those to whom they are sent. They are midwives in a process in which performative response, the birth-pangs of the hearer, is the goal, whether the contents of teaching are parabolic or immediately ethical.

NOTES

1 *The Parables of Jesus* (1976, of which the first, German, edition appeared in 1947), by Joachim Jeremias, laid the groundwork for future investigations.

2 In a section entitled 'Realized Discipleship', Jeremias called attention to the parables of the treasure in the field and the pearl (Matt. 13.44–6; Thomas 109, 76; Jeremias [1976], 198–201).

3 Jeremias discusses the parable of the merciful Samaritan in the same section (pp. 202–5).

4 The section on discipleship appears within a larger chapter, 'The Message of the Parables of Jesus' (pp. 115–229).

5 He borrows the phrase 'realized eschatology' from C. H. Dodd (pp. 117–18).

6 Jeremias (1976), pp. 120, 124.

7 ibid., pp. 128–32; cf. pp. 151–2.

8 When Jeremias deals with parables of a more explicitly eschatological nature, his christological predilection is kept in abeyance. 'The imminence of catastrophe', as depicted in them (pp. 160–9), functions as a 'call to repentance' (p. 169), and the threat that 'it may be too late' (pp. 169–80) underlines that call. Indeed, Jeremias' exegesis of the parables which depict 'the challenge of the hour' (pp. 180–98) permits him to speak of ethics without formally invoking the category of discipleship. He sees in the parable of the 'unjust steward', who might better be described as a clever manager (see Chilton, *Rabbi* [1984], pp. 117–23), that Jesus portrayed his hearers as people in a position of such crisis that immediate, by normal standards unscrupulous, action was called for (pp. 181–2). But even within this section, Jeremias reverts to his favourite theme. He takes the parable of the return of the unclean spirit (Matt. 12.43–45b/Luke 11.24–6) to mean that any possessed person ('house') must have 'the word of Jesus' as his 'rule of life', and must be pervaded by 'the joy of the kingdom', to avoid a fate worse than the initial possession (pp. 197–8). The order of those two imperatives is just as Jeremias presents them, although there is exegetical warrant for neither. When pressed by a passage which is difficult of interpretation, his reflex is to refer to discipleship, with the Kingdom taken as little more than a cipher for the call to follow Jesus.

9 p. 229; 'kingliness', as in earlier editions, would be a better rendering of '*Herrlichkeit*' than 'glory'; cf. (1977), p. 227.

10 See his *Commentary on Matthew's Gospel* 14.7, where Jesus is so identified, after the assertion that he is 'wisdom itself', 'righteousness itself', and 'truth itself', because he is the 'king of heaven'.

11 Linnemann (1966), p. xiii.

12 ibid., pp. 30–3.

13 ibid., pp. 33–41; the original edition of Jeremias' work (1947), p. 15, uses the phrase, which becomes '*Ort im Leben Jesu*' in later editions, cf. (1954), p. 16, (1976), p. 23, (1977), p. 19.

14 ibid., pp. 39–40.

15 As Linnemann herself puts the matter, 'Everywhere that men believe, Jesus is recognized as the one who has authority to speak and act in the name of God' (p. 41).

16 Via (1967), p. 55.

17 ibid., pp. 56–7.

18 ibid., pp. 89–93.

19 ibid., pp. 94–107.

20 ibid., p. 182.

21 ibid., pp. 193–4.

22 ibid., p. 197.

23 ibid., p. 203.

24 Crossan (1973), p. 82.

25 ibid., pp. 83–120.

26 In *Die rabbinischen Gleichnisse und der Gleichniserzähler Jesus* (1981).

27 Flusser, ibid., pp. 18–19.

28 Flusser dubs his method as 'structuralism, rightly understood' (p. 19). He has no evident interest in structure as a trans-cultural phenomenon of language, or as a paradigm within the human mind. That philosophical application of structuralism has, of course, won many adherents, but its exegetical value is extremely limited. The quest for the deep structure of language or mind which a text manifests treats the text as a mere symptom which evidences the use of options taken from the linguistic system to which it belongs. The text is only possessed of meaning in so far as it partakes of that systemic structure of language; for that reason, structuralists are more concerned with hypothetical structures than with particular texts (cf. T. K. Seung [1982] and Philip Pettit [1975]). Exegesis, on the other hand, is concerned with the meaning of individual texts, as autonomous expressions within definable contexts. The issue of an underlying structure is not exegetical, but philosophical or hermeneutical: exegetes simply exceed their competence when they move beyond the question of what texts, as texts, mean. When Flusser refers to 'structuralism, rightly understood', he focuses his reader's attention on the indisputable fact that parables were current within early Judaism, and argues that Jesus' distinctive technique is better understood by comparing his parables with those of his near contemporaries (pp. 19–21).

29 ibid., pp. 26–8, 65–6, 107–8, 141–4, 225, 257–8, 265–79. Although his volume is not anything like as comprehensive as that of Jeremias, and suffers from notable deficiencies (most obviously, in his handling of the Synoptic Problem), his is the most independent and significant study since Jeremias'. It is the innovative, and at the same time mature, product of long and diligent investigation.

30 ibid., pp. 26–7, 33, 145–6. He also uses the term 'epigonal' in respect
of such material.

31 ibid., pp. 33, 38–40.

32 ibid., pp. 33, 35, 156, 161–75, 177–92.

33 See *Shabbath* 153a, here paraphrased, and Flusser (1981), p. 23.

34 As Flusser points out (p. 37), the motif of the festal banquet appears
frequently in Jewish parables, and the basic structure of what we have
called narrative metaphor is shared by Jesus' parable and Yoḥanan's.

35 See Jeremias (1976), pp. 33, 67–9; and Flusser (1981), pp. 66–7.

36 Flusser, ibid., p. 26.

37 ibid., pp. 177–92, especially 187. He does so deliberately, under the
influence of the Russian formalist, Viktor Schklowskij (to whom
frequent reference is made in Flusser's volume). For Flusser, a motif
is the smallest narrative (or, as he would say, 'epic') unit in a parable,
and the 'theme' (or 'chief theme') is the primary motif (in this case,
a wedding) used in the parable. The 'subject' (spelled after the French
manner, which is the fashion among formalists), on the other hand,
does not refer to the contents of the parable, but to the point which
emerges from the way in which the motifs are constructed (pp. 36–7).
In so employing formalistic vocabulary, Flusser's analysis becomes
complex and somewhat confusing. What he calls the subject, the
informing impetus behind and through a parable, might better be
called its theme. Indeed, Flusser makes just that equation (p. 36).

38 This is an aspect to which Flusser refers, but does not undertake to
describe (see pp. 258, 278–9).

39 See Flusser, ibid., p. 24, and the *Semaḥoth of Rabbi Ḥiyya* 3; cf.
Michael Higger (1931), p. 221.

40 As Flusser points out (pp. 123–4).

41 cf. Jeremias (1976), pp. 146–53.

42 Flusser regards the parables mentioned within this paragraph as the
only ones which, in Jesus' preaching, treated of God's Kingdom (p.
65). His judgement rests on two, in this instance, shaky foundations.
On the basis of a general survey, he asserts that references (or allusions)
to the Kingdom in other parables are secondary insertions (pp. 66–
117). The principal criterion of his judgement is that, in parables other
than those specified, the reference to the Kingdom is not consistently
maintained in the Synoptic tradition. Seldom has the criterion of
'multiple attestation', which is only one of an array of criteria for
distinguishing the sayings of Jesus from later interpretations of them
(see R. H. Stein [1983], pp. 225–63), been elevated to a position of
such pre-eminence. Even if it be accepted in general terms, a singly
attested element might, on analysis, appear to be historically reliable,
as Flusser himself elsewhere acknowledges (pp. 193–233). In view of
the centrality of the Kingdom to Jesus' entire position, any jejune
dismissal of reference to it appears unwise. That observation brings us
to the second ground of Flusser's judgement: he understands Jesus'
self-realizing eschatology of the Kingdom to exclude a futuristic aspect

within it (pp. 64, 172). He admits that Jesus referred to such unequivocally eschatological images as God's festal meal, but argues that Jesus' conception of the Kingdom was not relevant to them (pp. 66-7). In so pressing the case of a realized definition of the Kingdom in Jesus' preaching (see pp. 41, 106, where alternative, non-eschatological contexts are devised), Flusser takes no cognizance of its normally eschatological emphasis in early Jewish theology. His attempt to exclude the bulk of Jesus' parables as metaphors of the Kingdom is therefore unsuccessful. Flusser nonetheless performs a useful service in drawing our attention to Jesus' parables of growth. What is problematic is giving them absolute pre-eminence, and interpreting them outside the context of eschatology, as C. H. Dodd did before Flusser; cf. Chilton, *Kingdom* (1984), pp. 10-11.

43   Flusser, ibid., pp. 37, 65.

44   ibid., pp. 150-1. He does not argue for any Hellenistic influence on Jesus in particular; the comparison is rather offered within the general programme of suggesting, in a tentative manner, that Jewish parables as a whole have analogies within Greek sources (pp. 141-60).

45   Perhaps some intimation of the distinctively eschatological aspect of Jesus' parable prompts Flusser's odd assertion that it might be secondary (pp. 150-1). The scholarly consensus is against him (cf. Jeremias [1976], pp. 151-3); Jesus' eschatological orientation is recognized nearly universally.

46   cf. Chilton, *Rabbi* (1984), pp. 60-1.

47   cf. Flusser (1981), pp. 141f. and Gereboff (1979), pp. 240-1.

48   Flusser, ibid., pp. 143-4. He cites Luke 5.10; Mark 1.17; Matt. 4.19 by way of comparison, in addition to Matt. 9.37-8; Luke 10.2 (pp. 141, 143); we have already called attention to the similar motif in John 4.35-8; Matt. 20.1-16.

49   Sanders (1985), pp. 11, 98-106.

50   See Ben F. Meyer (1979).

51   Although the matter cannot concern us directly here, it is notable that Jesus commissioned some of his followers to promulgate, and act upon, his own message. Classically, a disciple (*talmid*) within Judaism was expected to learn from his master, not to represent him. A *shaliah* (to which the Greek noun for apostle is probably related) might represent anyone, not only a rabbi, in a specific matter, much as a lawyer today might, but to commission followers as formal representatives of his teaching was an unusual step for Jesus to take (see C. K. Barrett [1978], pp. 88-102). It suggests that his message was particularly urgent, and that widespread response to that message was seen as a priority.

52   Sanders (1985), pp. 106-13.

53   ibid., p. 109.

54   ibid., p. 283.

55   ibid., pp. 187, 199, 206-7, 227.

56   ibid., p. 111.

57 See Jeremias (1979), pp. 485–502.
58 Sanders, ibid., p. 111.
59 ibid., pp. 109, 113.
60 ibid., pp. 112, 322.
61 ibid., p. 323.
62 The latter metaphor, of course, was even more challenging in its original context, where children were regarded less as innocent than as irresponsible, as comparable to the disabled; cf. *Shabbath* 153a and Albrecht Oepke (1978), pp. 636–54.

3

The Theology of the Kingdom

A phrase such as 'Kingdom of God' does not occur in a vacuum; it presupposes a symbolic world from which it derives theological meaning and significance. Within the symbolic world of the Gospels, its main thrust is dynamic strength, even active intervention.[1] It is misrepresented if it is given merely a geographical connotation, and devitalized if it is transposed into abstract categories, such as reign, rule, sovereignty or lordship – not to speak of even more remote theological terminology. Given dynamic performance by particular agents in specific contexts, it affects the lives of all those who engage with it, whether the original hearers or the modern readers: all are invited to join in the action by responding to God's incursion into their lives at the present moment of encounter, and by allowing themselves to be reoriented to God's future, his Kingdom in its fullness.

If this description of its operation is even partly justified, then the theology of the Kingdom stands near the heart of the epoch-making ministry of Jesus. Yet in this vital area, critical scholarship has not always succeeded in illuminating the central issues. As E. Schillebeeckx puts it, 'There is a sudden and complete dearth of references, the "critical apparatus" shrinks to nothing, at the very moment when it comes to dealing with the heart of Jesus' message...'[2] The reason, Schillebeeckx suggests, is that Jesus himself does not define his use of the term but rather allows its 'concrete content' to emerge 'from his ministry and activity as a whole, his parables and actual conduct'.[3] This, however, may be only one reason – although an important one – for the apparent failure to identify the epicentre of the earthquake. Another may lie in critical research itself, which has tended to transpose the material into forms which effectively bypassed the primary concern. For most of the twentieth century, the priority for the critics has been to determine whether Jesus' prophetic, poetic and parabolic utterances about the Kingdom constitute 'consistent' eschatology, or give evidence of 'realized' eschatology. Such determinations, in James Mackey's phrase, 'only tempt the modern mind, already too prone to literal interpretation, to mistake the very nature of symbolism'.[4] The use of symbolism and myth demands that we attend to the language and imagery in which they find expression and allow ourselves to be absorbed into their world. The language of the Kingdom brings the symbolic world to particular expression and performance, enabling the audience to participate more fully in its meaning and opening up issues that demand action. The approach adopted in this chapter is, therefore, to look first at the symbolic world which gives meaning to the Kingdom in ancient Israel and Judaism, taking account of the dialectic between the symbolic world as a whole and the distinctive performances of it; and then to look at the symbolic world of the Synoptic Gospels, which informs Jesus' performance of the Kingdom and is in turn informed by it.

1   THE KINGDOM IN ISRAEL'S SYMBOLIC WORLD

The symbol of the Kingdom in Israel is complex. No attempt can be made here to give a definitive or comprehensive account of it: we must be content simply to illustrate its leading characteristics. The subject is therefore presented as a series of cameos, each delineating a chosen feature.

(i) 'YAHWEH IS KING.' Most of the Old Testament references to Yahweh as King describe him as creator, King of the universe, victor over the chaos monster, and sustainer of the earth by his providence. In short, they are concerned with a creation theology which is fundamental to the Kingdom in Israel's symbolic world. It is no doubt possible to demonstrate an affinity between this kind of theology and divine kingship in ancient Near Eastern mythology.[5] More to the point, however, is the way in which the kingship of Yahweh was affirmed in Israel. It is implicit in the creation story in the first chapter of Genesis, in which Yahweh gives 'dominion' to man over the created order: a stewardship, not an absolute authority, for 'dominion' derives ultimately from Yahweh himself.[6] The 'enthronement' Psalms express the divine kingship in the context of cultic celebration.

> Declare among the nations, 'The Lord is King.
> He has fixed the earth firm, immovable;
> he will judge the peoples justly.'[7]

Since he is king of all the earth, he renews the earth's fertility and preserves its order and stability. In such psalms, the creation theology combines with other motifs: to 'judge the peoples justly' suggests the tradition of the covenant, which is discussed below. Nevertheless, the creation strand provides a critical balance to the more limited 'Israel' theology and preserves the idea of divine sovereignty over the entire cosmos. Later, it is evident in apocalypticism, which is really the old chaos/creation conflict transferred into the future. It is explicit in the devotions of Judaism. Indeed, it is the element which enabled Judaism to survive the collapse of apocalyptic hopes and praise 'the King of the universe who bringeth forth good from the earth'. It is represented in much of the Kingdom language in the Gospels and in Revelation.

(ii) 'WE HAVE NO KING BUT YAHWEH.' The roots of this tradition are probably to be found in the treaty terminology of the covenant: the Great King and his vassal. Associated with it is the ancient idea of Yahweh as warrior, the Lord of Hosts, which provides the context for the place of the Ark and the practice of holy war in the traditions of Israel, though the title 'king' is not frequently used in this connection.

Patterns of kingship in surrounding nations and the relative success of these kingdoms on the battlefield or in diplomacy led to increasing pressure on Israel's unwieldy amphictyony to accommodate the institution of kingship within its power structures.[8] In this social and political context, Gideon's claim has a defiant ring: 'I will not rule over you, and my son will not rule over you; the Lord (Yahweh) will rule over you' (Judg. 8.22f.). Theologically, this rejection of dynastic rule is an affirmation of the transcendent nature of the Kingdom in Israel, and in that sense 'the first shudder of eschatology'.[9] The Kingdom does not originate with, nor is it controlled by, human agents. It relates directly to political and communal concerns but is not a product of them. It is dynamic and invasive, and finds charismatic performance at the behest of the Spirit (*ruaḥ*) of Yahweh.

In consequence, the Kingdom is implicit in the recital of the 'mighty acts' wrought by Yahweh in the midst of his people: the sacred history (*Heilsgeschichte*) which informed Israel's cult and gained expression in its recited confessions or credos.[10] But, just as the covenant tradition penetrated creation theology, so also creation theology permeated the sacred history and provided it with a cosmic setting. The mighty act of deliverance at the Sea of Reeds is celebrated as nothing less than victory over watery chaos (Exod. 15.5,8); and Egypt, the oppressor of the children of Israel, is equated with the monster Rahab (Isa. 30.7; Ps. 89.10f.). Yet although this confluence of traditions lends depth to the story, it is useful to distinguish the individual strands conceptually when attempting to identify the principal elements that make up the symbol of the Kingdom in Israel.

(iii) 'YOU ARE MY SON: TODAY I HAVE BEGOTTEN YOU.' The fact that kings did come into being in Israel as 'the anointed of Yahweh' gives a remarkable new twist to the notion of sovereignty. Indeed, out of the tension between the old idea of Yahweh's dynamic kingship and the new 'monarchic unification' there grew 'a crisis of the theocratic impulse itself'.[11] Although generalization is hazardous,[12] it is clear enough that, faced with severe external pressures, Israel's political and strategic aim was to secure permanent, not occasional, leadership for the defence of its borders. Consequently, the theological axis was no longer primarily one of intermittent invasions (although Saul and David have their charismatic moments) but of permanent – if conditional – endowment, which received expression through cultic anointing, in which a covenant motif is apparent.[13] Thus the attempt was made to safeguard Yahweh's kingship, while Yahweh laid on the holder of the sacral office responsibility for the performance of his Kingdom in Israel.[14] But the transcendent kingship had been brought dangerously close to being commuted into the kingdom of Israel, with the power vested in a royal dynasty. Some hint of 'transcendental reserve' is detectable in Nathan's speech to David in 2 Sam. 7.5ff.: Would David indeed presume to build a house for Yahweh to dwell in? But the *Heilsgeschichte* culminates in this remarkable prophetic oracle: 'Your house and your kingdom shall be made sure for ever before me; your throne shall be established for ever' (2 Sam. 7.16; cf. Ps. 89.19–37). The transcendent horizon which the *Heilsgeschichte* provides seems here to confirm rather than check a triumphant imperialism (Ps. 2.8–11). The observation that a 'certain tension with the Sinaitic covenant and its stipulations, and thus with normative Yahwism, was perhaps inevitable'[15] is a studied understatement. The issue is clear: can the sovereignty of Yahweh find meaningful expression or performance through human dynastic rule? The affirmation that it does so underlies the notion of Davidic kingship, which in turn provided an important basis of messianic expectation in later times (see cameo v. below).

(iv) ' YOU ARE THE MAN.'   In face of the temptations of power, the transcendent aspect of the Kingdom of God had to be constantly reasserted on behalf of the Mosaic tradition.[16] The same prophet whose oracle seemed to underwrite dynastic power also gave performance to the judgement of God in the parable of the poor man's lamb (2 Sam. 12.1–6). By the skilful use of narrative the prophet creates a situation in which David becomes a participant even to the point of passing judgement on the 'rich man' in the parable – only to discover that he himself is the man in question (12.7). This is more than a personal rebuke. It is an affirmation by the prophet of the inseparability of eschatology and ethics: for if Yahweh, through his gracious covenant with Israel (cf. 2 Sam. 7.8ff.) has brought his people to the point where David is their anointed vassal-king, then David is required to be compassionate and to act for the oppressed, rather than as oppressor (cf. 12.6). Indeed, as the king in Israel diverges from the way of Yahweh, the demand that proceeds from Yahweh's righteous will is given explosive expression in prophetic utterance. 'The Lord roars from Zion' (Amos 1.2):

against the barbarism of the nations, the disobedience of Judah and the oppression and corruption of Israel. The King of creation and covenant breaks into the closed world of his people in judgement against the royal, priestly, legal and merchant establishment. We find here not simply the eschatology of impending catastrophe: there is a clear moral demand, which is couched in terms of the divine requirement for justice and righteousness and which speaks for the poor. No cultic offering, however elaborate, can be a substitute for this primary moral requirement. Amos was banished, never more to prophecy at Bethel, for, as Amaziah tells him with unconscious irony, 'it is the king's sanctuary, and it is a temple of the kingdom' (Amos 7.13).

(v) 'A SHOOT FROM THE STUMP OF JESSE.' Catastrophe came, and the pretensions of Israel's kingdom were exploded by Assyrian and Babylonian alike. The judgement of God had come on Israel not only in prophetic enactment but in historical disaster. Yet the prophets who taught Israel to interpret events in this way also invoked the notion of the divine King working in history. Even before Jerusalem crashed in ruins, the establishment of the divine Kingdom in the future was connected with the mission of a kingly agent on earth: the ideal 'son of David'.[17] In this perspective, the Kingdom is predominantly futuristic. But Yahweh is already in action for the salvation of his people. So all-embracing is the divine invasion of history that even a pagan emperor can be named as God's instrument,[18] and all nations be enlightened by Israel's faith (Isa. 49.6). The Gentiles are no longer potential enemies to be overcome; they are people in need of God's law. The rebuilt temple re-affirms the presence of Yahweh in their midst as King (cf. Zeph. 3.15). But there are indications now that the service of the king is the reverse of triumphalist. The so-called Servant Songs suggested that if Israel was to be Yahweh's ideal servant,[19] the way to victory would lie through uncomplaining and sacrificial service. The 'day of small things' (cf. Zech. 4.10) mocked over-facile expectations of the splendour soon to be (cf. Hag. 2.7).

The desperate days of Greek-Seleucid rule brought the revolt led by the Maccabees, which afforded at least a partial sense of achievement, and bequeathed a tradition of revolutionary zeal and martyrdom to Israel that effectively placed a time-bomb under the Roman occupation. At the same time it released some of the tensions engendered by what Buber called 'the paradox of theocracy'. Attention now focused on effective action on earth, and therefore on the divine agent. The scene was set for the revival of the ideal Davidic figure. But there are different nuances, as well as different degrees, in messianism.

The Hasmoneans themselves, who combined royal and priestly offices, contributed to the currency of the expectation of the priest-king (cf. Test. Lev. 18), but the offices are kept separate elsewhere in the Testaments of the XII Patriarchs and at Qumran. The model followed by the latter seems to have been that, while Israel will be governed by the elect high-priest of Aaron's line who would counsel the prince or king, the most important element was that the kingship be renewed.[20] The differentiation of priestly and kingly roles probably strengthened the Davidic character of the latter: there are several explicit references in the commentaries to the 'branch of David',[21] and the Benediction of the Prince of the Congregation (IQS[b]) clearly indicates a royal leader.[22]

The *locus classicus* for Davidic messianism, however, is Psalms of Solomon 17 and 18. Here the figure delineated is by no means simply a revolutionary. In Psalm 17 in particular, the Davidic king (17.21) is the latter-day fulfilment of the Davidic covenant (cf. 2 Sam. 7.1–17): a righteous king leading a people cleansed of unrighteousness (17.32). The emphasis is on God's king: it is God who will be King for ever and ever (17.1, 3, 40). 'The author was, evidently, more concerned with the great contrast to be expected from the radical change in history than with a detailed description of the period that was to ensue. And what really mattered was not the person of a particular king but the renewal of God's kingship through the house of David.'[23] The same point could be made in relation to the fourteenth benediction of the *Shemone Esre* (Palestinian recension), which prays for 'the kingdom of the house of David, your anointed one'. And the point will not be missed that this expectation is built into the prayer life of Israel, 'the least academic, and at the same time, most normative form'.[24]

Undoubtedly, symbols of this kind are 'plurisignificant': different people, interpreting them in different situations, find different nuances.[25] We do well not to identify Davidic messianism *simpliciter* with the political revolutionaries and rebels against the Roman *imperium*, but to recognize at the same time that the symbol invariably implied 'purging Jerusalem from nations that trample her down to destruction' (Ps. Sol. 17.23–32). Not all Jewish groups were equally sympathetic to the implied political *praxis* (the Sadducees of the temple establishment were among the more resistant), but it was clearly so pervasive about the time of Jesus that it was impossible to avoid contact with it in Israel. When messianism came to be interpreted in relation to a particular figure, the rabbinic movement tended to become polarized. R. Akiba hailed Simon bar Kokhba ('Son of the Star', a messianic title derived from Num. 24.17, the star out of Jacob) as king Messiah. R. Yoḥanan ben Torta replied drily, 'Akiba, grass will grow out of your cheek-bones before the son of David comes'.[26]

(vi) VISIONS SEEN IN THE NIGHT. Apocalyptic literature has certain readily definable characteristics, which include anonymous or pseudonymous authorship, the use of dreams and visions, panoramas in the form of *vaticinia ex eventu* (lit. prophecies arising out of the happening itself, or prophecies after the event), symbolic language to which its audience has the key, and esoteric content.[27] Creatively imaginative and inventive, its purpose was usually to strengthen the resolve of its readers. The apocalyptic book of Daniel has been described as 'non-violent resistance literature' addressed to Jews suffering persecution at the hands of Antiochus IV Epiphanes; in return for their loyalty to their religious traditions it promises 'eternal life by means of resurrection in the new age', i.e., the Kingdom of God.[28] Apocalypticism appeals to people *in extremis*: it reeks of disillusion with the world as it is, it trades in lurid technicolour images and has a fixated fascination with end-of-the-age dénouements. Hence it can well be ascribed 'to a failure of nerve, to the hypochondriac's penchant for exaggerating the evils of the age, to the coward's anxious search for an escape clause in humanity's contract with history'.[29] More positively, it witnesses to the human and religious longing for an end to brutality and hopelessness and for the coming of the new age that is in God's gift, when his purposes for his creation will reach fulfilment. It is to this end that it images forth the dramatic decision of God for the salvation and judgement of the world; a final action in which the people of God will share.

The seventh chapter of Daniel provides ample illustration of apocalyptic method and its implication for the Kingdom. The vision is of four beasts whose origin is primeval watery chaos.[30] The cipher is not obscure: the beasts are the successive empires which have devoured and oppressed Israel, with a special last place ('the little horn') reserved for Antiochus IV Epiphanes. The beasts are superseded, the fourth (and worst!) being despatched outright, and the Ancient of Days (i.e., the Ancient One, in contrast to the ephemeral upstarts) gives 'dominion, glory and Kingdom' to 'one in human likeness'.[31]

The 'son of man' symbol has long been a *cause célèbre* in the study of Christian origins, and in this connection the ancestry of Daniel's human-like figure has been traced to the Man-King mythology of the Near East as well as to a variety of other sources.[32] It is more important, however, to follow out the inner logic of Daniel's image: there is the divine tribunal over which the Ancient One presides, attended by myriad angels (7.9f.);[33] there are the beasts, representing the *earthly* kingdoms which are deprived of their power;[34] the 'one in human likeness', who comes 'with clouds of heaven' (as opposed to the earth or watery chaos from which the beasts came), is presented before the Ancient One and is given the kingdom, universal and eternal (7.14). What does this symbolize? By an accepted literary device, an angel of the heavenly court explains to Daniel: unlike the four earthly kings, the holy ones of the Most High 'shall receive the kingdom and possess the kingdom for ever...' (7.18; cf. 7.27). The Kingdom given to them will not be superseded in the cyclical rhythm that bears all earthly kingdoms to destruction and oblivion, but is imperishable and all-embracing. The faithful who continue for the time being to suffer on earth are thus encouraged to identify with Daniel's apocalyptic dream-world, fortified by the thought that the secret 'wisdom' they share pronounces the term and doom of their oppressors and gives assurance of their own eternal compensation.

(vii) THE WAR TO END ALL WARS.   Related to the visions of the end is the vivid portrayal of 'the battle for the destruction of the sons of darkness' – a time of the greatest tribulation 'from its sudden beginning until its end in eternal redemption':[35] 'to the God of Israel shall be the kingdom, and among the saints of his people will he display might'.[36] In the apocalyptic world view, the faithful community is itself 'eschatological' and the events in which it is involved are therefore the final events. Heroism and fanaticism combine in a self-sacrificing devotion that is part of the birth-pangs of the new age. Monocular vision of this kind is the stuff of tragedy – or pathetic folly. In such an apocalyptic scenario the Kingdom is embedded. It appears as Satan is overthrown and sorrow banished (as in the typically pseudonymous Assumption of Moses). The final action is precipitated by the Heavenly One arising from his royal throne to execute judgement on the wicked, including the Gentiles, and to bring happiness to Israel.

(viii) 'MAY HE ESTABLISH HIS KINGDOM – SPEEDILY.' The normal life of Judaism, apart perhaps from exceptionally critical episodes, was relatively disengaged from the more extreme forms of apocalypticism, even if not entirely insulated against them. The two principal matrices in post-exilic Judaism were the Torah (cf. Neh. 8.1–8) and the temple cult (cf. Ezek. 40—48). Both nurtured the believing community in the service of God, whose kingdom is discernible in past and present and looked for in the future. There thus emerged a genuine dialectic between eschatology and ethics. The symbol of the Kingdom issues in moral performance, i.e., in the service that impinges on every aspect of the believers' being and life-style. Sometimes, as in Jubilees 23.26f., the impression is given of the realization of the Kingdom by stages.[37] In the synagogues, the Kaddish prayer suggests the longing for, indeed the expectation of, the speedy and complete establishment of the Kingdom:

> Magnified and sanctified be his great name in the world that he has created according to his will.
> May he establish his kingdom in your lifetime and in your days and in the lifetime of all the house of Israel, even speedily and at a near time.

The corollary is that in this present time one responds to God as King by doing his will. The parallel in the Lord's Prayer is hardly accidental.[38] Indeed, at least from the second century AD onwards, the synagogue faithful took upon themselves 'the yoke of the Kingdom' (or 'the yoke of the Torah') in morning and evening prayer. To take the yoke of the Kingdom meant submission to God as King now (as opposed to being 'stiff-necked') and, in terms of Lev. 20.26, to set oneself apart from wrongdoing.[39] Thus harnessed to the service of the Kingdom, the faithful are to respond in love to God 'wholeheartedly', be ready to lay down their lives for the Kingdom ('with all your soul') and put all their resources (*mamon*) at its disposal ('with all your might': cf. Deut. 6.4f.). B. Gerhardssohn has described this as the transformation of 'the ethos of theocracy' into 'the ethos of the children of God, the secret of which lies not in external laws and ritualized patterns of behaviour but in people's hearts'.[40] The difficulty is that abstractions such as 'the ethos of theocracy' are inadequate to express the dynamism of the Kingdom, while response to it is somewhat more than a matter of internalizing law and ritual.

A brief survey of eight cameos of 'the Kingdom of God' in Israel cannot claim to be a definitive discussion, but certain general observations may be permissible. Clearly, each particular age or epoch tended to have a dominant expression of the Kingdom, asserted over against opposition: Gideon's theocratic charisma, over against the compromising of Israel's heritage from the desert; Nathan's insistence on the claims of morality over against the ruthlessness of incipient totalitarianism; messianism over against resigned fatalism, and so on. But, as the strains and tensions indicate, the dominant expressions are not universally held. Antimonarchical tendencies persist during the monarchy;[41] rampant apocalypticism coexists with the quiet pietism of people like Simeon, 'righteous and devout, looking for the consolation of Israel' (Luke 2.25). Yet most of these conflicting tendencies reflected some aspect(s) of Israel's symbolic world, which is therefore seen to possess a certain fluidity. Different people may activate the same symbol in different ways: not merely through individualism or the human penchant for rationalization, but also because symbols are genuinely polyvalent – 'king' meant something quite different to Gideon and to Solomon, or to Elijah and Jezebel. Religious symbols, and most others too, are 'plurisignificant', in Norman Perrin's phrase; 'they can never be exhausted in any one apprehension of meaning'.[42] Within the wide parameters of Israel's symbolic world, it may be said that 'the reign of God means what its users make it to mean; it does not have a set meaning by which all users are expected to abide'.[43]

A possible conclusion from our cameos is that both parameters and creative imagination are important factors in engendering symbolic meaning. The parameters provide certain pointers to the nature of the Kingdom: it is always transcendent, never to be manipulated by the users if it is to remain valid; it is dynamic, exploding into meaning and creating new possibilities; it opens out in the form of human performance, uniting eschatology and ethics. Those who see furthest into its range of meaning are those, like the prophets, who have been given insight and sensitivity into the mystery of God's ways. In the New Testament, Jesus possesses such sensitivity to a remarkable degree and brings together elements from the given symbolic world into new and exciting motifs, opening up issues and possibilities of far-reaching consequence.

2 THE KINGDOM IN JESUS' SYMBOLIC WORLD

(i) THE PRELUDE: JOHN THE BAPTIST. Amid the fluidity and turbulence of Jewish eschatological expectation and apocalyptic speculation, John the Baptist acted – in Christian terms – as an important theological catalyst. In the apparent forefront of his message was the invasive Kingdom of God, characterized as imminent and making an impact accordingly on the popular consciousness.[44] Apart from his use of the 'summons to repentance' or the 'summons to flee' (Matt. 3.7–10; Luke 3.7ff.), the form of his message was not precisely paralleled in earlier prophecy.[45] Being determined by the message itself, it was essentially the announcement of imminent, messianic salvation/judgement.[46] Eschatological imminence (its leading edge) cohered in triangular fashion with moral and spiritual preparedness (its leading theme) and with the practice of baptism (its cultic issue): a powerful syndrome, inaugurating a movement of national repentance (its ethical issue). If the language of the Kingdom was indeed employed, then it referred to the performance of the Kingdom in a proleptic way: the imminent Kingdom was already having effect on the human scene. The prolepsis was explicit in the triple tests of messianic times – water, wind (*ruah, pneuma*) and fire[47] – of which John claimed to perform only the first: 'possibly a novel adaptation of proselyte baptism'.[48] Admittedly, Christian tradition relating to John is so laden with interpretative imagery that the problem of John's self-consciousness is almost as intractable as that of Jesus.[49] Indeed, it is even possible that John did not frame his message in terms of God's Kingdom. One can, however, separate out in general terms John the prophet of the imminent 'coming', who is contextualized in the environment and thought-world of first-century Judaism (including Qumran and other baptist movements), and John the forerunner of the Messiah in conventional Christology (cf. *Elijah redivivus*). Between the two is the assessment of John made by Jesus. The difficult logion in Matt. 11.12/Luke 16.16 probably originates with Jesus. If interpreted *in malam partem* (as it often is), its imagery might be derived from the world of apocalyptic described above, viz., the conflict of the sons of light and the sons of darkness:[50] the approach of the Kingdom to the 'real' world would then be characterized by violence, of which John is victim primarily at the hands of Herod Antipas.[51] If, however, it is held that this exegesis does violence to the text, it may be preferable to look behind the complex tradition which Matt. 11.12/Luke 16.16 represents and to discern, on the basis of linguistic evidence and tradition history, a primitive 'Q' saying which operated *in bonam partem*: 'the Kingdom of God avails itself, and everyone avails himself of it'.[52] The import of the saying would then be, 'before John, law; from then on, Kingdom'. Jesus announces that from the time of John, God comes in strength. 'Because he is making himself felt, there is no further need for legal mediation between God and man: we may enter his very presence because He is present with us.'[53] The time of fulfilment is at hand.

(ii) 'THE TIME IS FULFILLED.' Jesus' proclamation in Mark is that 'the *kairos* has reached its fulness' (1.15). The 'moment of truth' has burst upon the human scene, in the message of the 'nearness' of the Kingdom. The Kingdom 'intersects' time.[54] An area of overlap between the ministries of John and Jesus is discernible – indeed, in Matthew their initial message is identical (3.2; 4.17); not only John's ministry but his death foreshadows what will befall Jesus (cf. Mark 6.14–29).[55] But if Jesus' initial proclamation is of the 'imminence' of the Kingdom, the performance of the message, both in his preaching and teaching, effects the *present* 'crisis' in time, the 'moment of truth', the encounter with the Kingdom. The language of imminent approach subtly shades into that of present invitation. The Kingdom that intersects time is 'at hand' in the sense that it may be entered; it is a realm of meaning and existence into which one can move. Thus performance leads on to existential or ethical theme. In the Marcan formulation, the primary issue is the response of repentance and belief in the gospel. It is the twin theme of 'turning to God' and 'trusting in God'. Though transmitted in Marcan language, repentance is intrinsic to the logic of Jesus' performance of the Kingdom. To raise doubts about its authenticity, as Sanders does,[56] is to illustrate the shortcomings of the criterion of dissimilarity rather than to elucidate Jesus' message. It might be observed, tentatively and parenthetically, that the reason that Mark's narrative of the beginnings of Jesus' ministry is overlaid with interpretation and later terminology may be that it is essentially concerned with establishing perspective. His ministry is about fulfilment, the Kingdom, repentance and the good news. The subsequent narrative will show distinctive emphases in relation to these general themes.

The irruption of the Kingdom into history is accomplished through an agent who is essentially its performer. The performer articulates its motifs, conveys meaning and opens up issues. While articulating in words – preaching and teaching by 'the word' are central to his method, as is his audience's 'hearing' with insight and obedience – Jesus also gives performance to the Kingdom in dramatic action, which in turn opens up issues and possibilities for those involved. A performance characterized by 'power' (*exousia*: Mark 1.22, 27), it has manifest effects on the situation (1.27; 2.12): not only conveying verbal meaning but also something of the 'feel' of the Kingdom's dynamic power to effect God's will, evoking on the human side surprise, wonder, joy. Its effectiveness is in a particular direction: it is for healing, wholeness, *shalom*, sanity. Thus it strikes a blow at Satan's kingdom (3.23–7): 'I saw Satan fall like lightning from heaven' (Luke 10.18). It is as if Jesus has given performative expression, in the real conditions of his ministry, to the war of the sons of light and sons of darkness. Apocalyptic symbolism provides the motif for dramatic, parabolic action: 'If it is by the finger of God that I cast out demons then the Kingdom of God has come upon you' (Luke 11.20).[57]

If apocalyptic imagery denotes any reality, it is found not by reading the cipher of apocalypticism into current events of world history (cf. Mark 8.11f. par.) but by recognizing that Jesus has given performance to the apocalyptic drama before our very eyes: he has transposed the conflict between the ultimate duality of good and evil from the 'never-never' world of apocalyptic speculation into the real world of human experience. He has brought the Kingdom within our reach and created space for us to move into God's realm and feel its power. 'The Kingdom of God is in your midst' (*entos humon*: Luke 11.20f.): opening out around us, bidding us enter. There is thus a close relationship between miracle story and parable.[58] They are both performances of the motif of the new creation, the Kingdom of God, intersecting time and history. In this way the problematic relation between speech and reality receives clarification in terms of Jesus' own ministry. His statements do not stand *in vacuo*, as exhibitions of language without reference to external content, as if indeed there had never been anything but words:[59] 'Go and tell John what you hear and see...' (Matt. 11.4). Similarly, the parable of Satan's kingdom (Mark 3.23) interprets Jesus' exorcisms. The context, however, is Jesus' ministry – not his person and not Christology! And the message is constant: the moment of truth has arrived: the Kingdom is *entos humon*.

(iii) THE MYSTERY OF THE KINGDOM.   Mark understood Jesus to speak of the *musterion* of the Kingdom (4.11): a term which seems to combine the notion of 'transcendence' (i.e., that which transcends and therefore defies complete human comprehension) with that of the 'hidden' or 'secret', about which followers or disciples are given some 'inside' information or insight. It may carry other connotations, such as the power to disorientate or disconcert the safe, complacent world of the hearers (cf. 4.12), but of this more later. The mystery of the Kingdom, whatever it is, is conveyed in parables, though the human response to the parables may vary greatly (as in the 'interpretation' of the sower: 4.14-20). Why this apparent necessity for parable (4.33f.)? That is the first question for discussion.

Parables are clearly a teaching device, an imaginative projection of meaning, on Jesus' part: not his invention as far as the form is concerned, for the rabbis certainly used them, but the focusing of images, the performance of stories which present some kind of parallel with human life as his hearers knew it and suggest deeper levels of meaning which they could pursue but never exhaust. They move in the world of metaphor and symbol: indeed, they give expression, at least in part, to Jesus' symbolic world. In so far as the symbol assumes story form, it may be described by the *religionsgeschichtliche*[60] term, 'myth': 'the parables of Jesus are Jesus' own myth of the reign of God, as meal and prayer are its ritual, and service its life-style'.[61] But before we become embroiled in terminological controversy, it is well at this stage to look more closely at the parables themselves.

Ostensibly, parables – or many of them – are images or stories suggesting an element of 'comparison' with the Kingdom: 'With what can we compare the Kingdom of God, or what parable shall we use for it?' (Mark 4.30). To the Western mind at any rate, the temptation is to conclude that the parables are a 'concretizing' of the abstract idea of 'the Kingdom of God'. Or, if we were to apply the (basically Piagetian) terminology of the educationist Bruner, parables move the language of the Kingdom out of the purely symbolic realm into iconic representation: they 'picture' the operation of the symbol in a selected setting, just as so-called 'acted parables' – like table fellowship, feeding the multitude, acts of healing or the entry to Jerusalem – transpose the symbol yet again into 'enactive' expression. There is certainly some value in this kind of perspective, but it carries the danger of placing Jesus' parabolic operations in a straitjacket. For example, it would tend to suggest that Jesus was illustrating an abstract concept, viz., the Kingdom; or that the aim of parable was to impart knowledge of a difficult concept that would otherwise be beyond the grasp of the hearers (cf.

4.33). But it is clear that, generally speaking, this is not what he is doing. If it had been, his parables would have been iconic variations on the conceptual theme of 'the Kingdom': i.e., on the nature of the king and his rule. Only a few parables, and then only arguably, meet such a specification: perhaps the king at the last judgement (Matt. 25.34–46), the king who settles his accounts (Matt. 18.23–5) or more remotely, the king going into battle (Luke 14.31f.); even these in no way support the conclusion that parables are simply about the concretizing of the Kingdom symbol. Rather, the parables articulate and image a reality that can be discerned, encountered and responded to in the midst of life. The articulation and the imagery are therefore drawn from life. The Kingdom can be compared to the mysterious process of growth that calls for decisive human action at the critical moment, but is otherwise independent of human activity (Mark 4.26–9), or to the astonishing product of the tiny mustard seed (Mark 4.30ff.), or to the fate of seed sown in a field (Mark 4.3–9), or to the leavening process (Matt. 13.33; Luke 13.20f.), or to the budding fig-tree – a messianic parable (Mark 13.28f. par.). It may also be compared to the consequence of the sabotaging of a wheat field, and how the 'householder' deals with the weed-infested crops (Matt. 13.24–30). It is like finding treasure in a field (Matt. 13.44) or a pearl of great value (Matt. 13.45): in these circumstances, you know what you have to do! Again, it is like searching for a lost sheep (Matt. 18.12ff.; Luke 15.4–7) or a lost coin (Luke 15.8ff.): the joy on finding it is overwhelming. The motifs, or *tertia comparationis*, may be found in the complex world of human relations: employer–employee (e.g., Matt. 20.1–16; Matt. 25.14–30/Luke 19.12–27; Luke 17.7–10); the treatment of debtors (e.g., Luke 7.41ff.), and the payment of accounts (Matt. 18.23–35; Luke 16.1–8); the world of family and friends (e.g., Luke 11.5–8; 15.11–32; Matt. 21.28–32); social and religious division (Luke 10.25–37); religious attitudes in people (Luke 18.9–14); rich and poor (Luke 16.19–31); even children at play (Matt. 11.16–19; Luke 7.31–5). It does not matter that some parables are linked explicitly to the Kingdom and others not. It is evident that all are designed to name, to articulate, even to dramatize, some aspects of the reality of life in which everyone is involved, and to discern the activity of God in it. The thematic emphasis may be on watchfulness (cf.

Mark 13.34f.) against the burglar (Matt. 24.42ff.), but the setting may equally well be a wedding (Matt. 25.1–13); or it may be a question of precedence, but the setting a marriage feast (Luke 14.7–11). Hence the parables take the rich tapestry of life as the setting in which the Kingdom is manifested: not manifested, however, to the casual onlooker but to those who 'have eyes to see'. The truth has to be 'discerned' in the performance that is designed to focus attention on it. But the fact that it is discernible in God's creation, disturbed though it is by enemy action (cf. Matt. 13.28), suggests that creation is 'theonomous': that it is God's creation and God's hand is discernible in its working. Yet this is not by virtue of some 'natural law' that unlocks its veiled presence to rational scrutiny: it is so because of God's decision for his creation; it is so because the Kingdom, characteristically invasive, has already broken in upon the human scene – not least in the parabler and the parables he tells. The silence is broken. De-worded creation is speaking again. The Kingdom has emerged from dream-world and begun to convey its secrets through the world of experience. And the parables are the focus of its performance.

This brings us to the second major question. The performance of the parables has a depth of significance that takes it beyond a mere teaching method. That it *involves* a teaching method is not in dispute: 'With many such parables he spoke the word to them, as they were able to hear it' (Mark 4.33). The first hearing of a parable is a challenge to discern how it might engage one at a deeper level, as the enigmatic formula, 'He that hath ears to hear, let him hear', suggests. It is a challenge to embark on a voyage of exploration which may indeed bring one the joy of finding the pearl of great price, but it also entails the pain of leaving known ways, the disorientation entailed by leaving behind familiar landmarks, and the disconcertment of self-discovery. The performance of some parables is geared to disconcerting the audience immediately: the good Samaritan is a case in point (Luke 10.27–37). Others leave us to come to terms with uncomfortable implications for ourselves – for example, as we see something of our own reflection in the elder brother (Luke 15.25–32). More elusive parables demand a possibly lengthy process of reflection: some of the parables recorded in Mark 4 appear to be of this type. The general tendency of parables, however, is to confound our conventional and comfortable world view: to shake us out of complacency and imperviousness to the challenge of the Kingdom or the Word. Their demand is therefore far-reaching and more likely to be evaded than welcomed: enemy action is still effective!

Mark takes this problem by the scruff of the neck. Parables are designed to relate to 'those outside' the secret of the Kingdom (4.11): not, however, because 'outsiders must stay outside and be damned'.[62] Their purpose is precisely to face them with the baffling mystery of life: 'so that (*hina*) they may indeed see but not perceive, and may indeed hear but not understand...'. If the *hina* clause expresses purpose,[63] the disconcerting meaning would be that Jesus told parables in order that his message might not be understood. It appears, however, that this text presupposes the Targum of Isaiah 6.9, 10,[64] and this may serve to modify the purposive sense of *hina*. Mark is using – and representing Jesus as using – the mildly ironic Isa. 6.9f., in which the prophet conceives of his vocation as being a hopeless mission in terms of human success. The fact is that a prophetic ministry confronts people with uncomfortable choices, and the possibility of rejection is high. In Mark, the way forward is clearly indicated: it lies in *teshuvah* – 'lest they should turn again and *be forgiven*'. Here, Mark 4.12b again seems to reflect the Targum of Isaiah 6.10 rather than the Old Testament text: 'and they repent, and it be forgiven them'.[65] This is the point of intersection between the reality of the Kingdom and our present life-style: the parabolic incursion of the Kingdom that tears away our defences and shows us how to enter the Kingdom 'like a child' (cf. Mark 10.15). This is the sacrifice that is required before the pearl of great price is ours.

Matthew handles the problem in a different way, although it is recognizably the same problem. The question of teaching method is raised at the outset: 'Why do you speak to them in parables?' (Matt. 13.10). There is the same distinction between those to whom 'it has been given to know the secrets of the Kingdom' and those who have no such intimacy with it (13.11). Indeed, at this point he invokes the logion, 'to him that hath shall be given...' (13.12). The problem is to find oneself in the position to realize the gift. 'This is why I speak to them in parables', Matthew continues, '*because* (*hoti*) seeing they do not see...' (13.13). Isaiah's 'slightly disgusted irony' becomes Jesus' irony:[66] people are unwilling to pay the price of their own healing. But those who do – those who give themselves to the mystery of the Kingdom, as the disciples have done – are truly blessed (13.16). And Matthew takes the theme further. Many prophets and righteous men longed to see (hear) what you see (hear) and did not have the opportunity of doing so. Therefore, in the parabolic ministry of Jesus the mystery of the Kingdom is given performance in a way that is new: it enables the Kingdom to open out to our vision and understanding so that entry to it becomes a practical possibility *now*. Yet whenever this possibility emerges as real, there is a recognition that it has been 'given' (cf. 13.11f.): it is something that has not emerged from our own resources but has been brought about by the invasion of our lives by a new element, viz., the Kingdom of God. It is God's gracious gift to us.

The tailpiece to this discussion is that the 'insiders', such as the disciples, constantly undergo the disorientation of parabolic confrontation with the Kingdom. It is not a matter merely of a once-for-all *teshuvah*. Such a reorientation brings one to the point of entry. But growth within the mystery, the realization of the 'more' that is given, is not without its disconcertment. The disciples to whom the secret is said to be given constantly fail to understand: 'Do you not understand this parable? How then will you understand all the parables?' (Mark 4.13). Mark explores the theme of the disciples' misunderstanding and failure much more explicitly than Matthew, building it up into a major strand in the gospel story, although it is possible to exaggerate Mark's negative view of the disciples;[67] Mark lays emphasis on the close fellowship that existed between Jesus and his disciples (cf. 4.34), suggesting a model of nurture-through-community in relation to the meaning of the parables and the mystery of the Kingdom. Misapprehension and disorientation were part of the learning process, rather than an indication that the disciples' tradition had run out into the sand.[68] There is an identifiable pedagogic, which operates through the dialectic of understanding and misunderstanding. Yet there is no guarantee that disorientation or alienation will prove of positive pedagogic value. In such a case, the encounter with Jesus becomes

judgement. It was so, apparently, in the clashes over forgiveness
(2.5–12), table fellowship (cf. 2.15–17) and the Sabbath (2.23–
36), when the reality of the Kingdom clashed with entrenched
religious prejudice of a theological, conventional or institutional
type. It was also the case, apparently, in the clash with the
Pharisees over the tradition of the elders (Mark 7.1–23). It was
so, certainly, in the coalition of political and religious self-
interest which led to Jesus' death (cf. 3.6; 11.8; 12.13). Indeed,
parabolic understanding could increase the enmity (12.12), for
parables 'may have corrosive effects on the oral unity of speaker,
message and hearers'.[69] They subvert, disturb and create paradox. It was otherwise with the disciples. Their repeated mis-
understandings about the loaves (6.37; 8.4; 8.17f.) represent a
narrative device which is also a form of pedagogy, depicted by
Mark in such bold and repetitive caricature that it conveys
simultaneously the impression of importance and riddle. The
paradox emerges that while Jesus' sufferings and death were the
toll exacted for the alienation of his enemies, they were also the
only way by which his disciples could come to a final appreciation of what his message really was.

It is time now to specify more clearly the relationship of
parables and Kingdom. Are the parables inducting the hearers
into the myth of the Kingdom?[70] Is it proper to speak, as C. H.
Dodd did,[71] of 'the parables of the Kingdom'? If so, in what
sense? Not in the sense that all the parables make explicit
reference to the Kingdom: as one critic has observed, there are
'only five authentic parables introduced explicitly' as parables
of the Kingdom, 'and in many instances there is suspicion that
the introduction is redactional'.[72] Dodd's work has established
a tradition of exegesis from which it is hard to break away.[73] Yet
it is important to question it. His 'realized eschatology', like its
successor 'inaugurated eschatology', belongs to a modern realm
of theological or ideological discourse, set in tension with the
'thoroughgoing eschatology' of Weiss and Schweitzer. As an
ideology, it has no real counterpart in the text of the Gospels:
Jesus did not argue for 'realized eschatology', any more than he
advocated or practised 'thoroughgoing eschatology'. As we
have already seen, he did not use parables to elucidate the
difficult concept of the Kingdom nor, incidentally, to reinforce
the myth of the Kingdom (as Perrin argued). Examination of the

parables suggests that Jesus challenged the Kingdom myths held by his contemporaries: whether these myths were essentially nationalistic, localized, cultic, legalistic or apocalyptic. If we compare the parables with the symbolic world of the kingdom of Israel, what is striking is how distinctive the world of the parables is. It is the world of everyday experience, incorporated into narratives that sometimes exaggerate and sometimes caricature but always 'tease the mind into active thought'.[74] 'When Jesus addressed his parables to those who fully accepted the myth of God as king, he was inviting them to surrender the associations they habitually made with the Kingdom of God.'[75] The point Breech misses, especially when he traces the source of realism in modern Western literature not simply to Mark (as Auerbach did) but to the parables of Jesus, is that Jesus is following prophetic precedent here. Nathan confronts the king of Israel, the pinnacle of Israel's power structure, with the simple story of rich man, poor man and a pet ewe lamb – and thereby says the unsayable, showing the king what it means to be king in Israel (2 Sam. 12.1–4): Jesus freely uses imagery from everyday life to express the inexpressible. The secret strategy of the parables, as Kelber put it,[76] is 'in all instances seduction by the ordinary with a view toward the extraordinary'. The logic of the parabolic method contains the implication that the 'mystery' of the Kingdom – the riddle of God's presence, power and purpose, and of human duty, value and goal – will unfold itself not in the systematic exploration of the myth or symbol of 'the Kingdom of God' but through reflection on and response to features of real life delineated and imaged in parable. It suggests that, under the surface even of the mundane and the ordinary, there lies a deeper reality, a richer order of meaning; and it is the particular genius of the parable to defy superficial and defensive readings by fracturing the surface of this deeper realm. It is a method which admits of variety of interpretation as the interpreter relates to the parable in his or her own life-situation (hence, parabolic 'polyvalence'); but there are also constraints on interpretation given in the structure of the parable itself.[77] In the freedom and firmness of parabolic engagement, we encounter the reality with which, as human beings, and (to use the 'Kingdom' metaphor) as God's subjects, we are primarily concerned.

What is it, at this deepest level, that we can yet discover with great joy to be the most precious thing we know, but that will then claim from us all that we have to give? It is life, obviously, it is existence itself, the very life and existence of ourselves and everything around us. To discover and rediscover life and existence, all life and all existence, as the most precious thing we know, always already there and offered for our acceptance, is to see life as a gift to us or, in the original meaning of the word, as grace. And nothing so much as a precious gift can claim our total responsibility, to cherish it infinitely, to do all in our power to maintain and enhance it, to be generous even as we ourselves have been so unstintingly enriched.[78]

(iv) JESUS AND THE KINGDOM.   Jesus the parabler is intimately related to the parables he told. Yet, as always in discussion of the parables, a qualification must be entered. There is a sense in which the parables point away from Jesus to themes located in life itself, in the midst of which the Kingdom of God is discerned. Yet Jesus is part of 'life itself', and in many important respects he lived out the parables. Any teller is implicitly involved in his tales, and some tellers play out their tales. Jesus belongs to the latter category. If the Kingdom is discerned in the interaction of people and world, Jesus himself is a catalyst of such interaction. If the Kingdom is discerned in the complex relationships of a father and two sons, Jesus is found welcoming the prodigal and agonizing over the elder brother. If the Kingdom involves overcoming prejudice and traditional barriers, Jesus operates at precisely this frontier. If the Kingdom is about sacrificing everything for the pearl of great price, we are left in no doubt that if anyone has realized the treasure it is Jesus. There is a sense in which, as his ministry unfolds, Jesus' lifestyle is itself parabolic. It comes as something of a shock, therefore, to note the symbols which are less prominent or are given only modified credence in relation to Jesus' performance of the Kingdom.

One is the messianic or christological. The paradox is intense, for Mark focused his introduction on Jesus as 'Christ' (i.e., 'anointed', 'Messiah': 1.1). Yet the qualification entered against messianic or christological symbolism at Caesarea Philippi is immense. Matthew, like the church he represented, insisted on celebrating Peter's good confession (16.17ff.), but this is clearly secondary. The Marcan qualifications remain at the centre of

the tradition: the command to be silent (8.30), the necessity for
Jesus to face rejection by the establishment and death at its
hands, and the completion of his ministry by 'rising again'
(8.31). This, says Mark, is given as a plain factual statement
(8.32) – with an indication that it is the living out in the
particularities of Jesus' ministry of the kind of response that is
required of every follower (8.34–7). Only within this context
is any credence given to christological symbolism. So important
is this perception to Mark and the Synoptic Evangelists that
they convey its import no less than three times (in the so-called
'passion predictions'), the unprecedented redundancy indicating that one finds here an essential perspective on Jesus'
ministry – and, indeed, on the Kingdom, for messianic ministry
is a major expression of the Kingdom in the tradition of Israel
(as we have seen above).[79] If Jesus therefore distances his
ministry from traditional views of messianic Kingdom, it follows
that his performance of the Kingdom cannot be interpreted
primarily in christological terms: rather, Christology has to be
understood in the light of his performance of the Kingdom.[80]
His ministry is now seen to follow a teleological pattern which
leads through suffering and death to the life of 'resurrection'.
Hence any attempt to capture the Kingdom of God within
worldly sovereignty or power – whether Zealotic or Caesarian –
will meet with either critical or ambivalent response, for the
transcendent factor qualifies the alleged realization: while not
denying worldly obligations, one always renders to God what
belongs to him – including the Kingdom ('only God is
King').

Other symbols subjected to severe qualification or rejection
include the apocalyptic. Mark uses apocalyptic material as an
important signpost in the second half of Jesus' ministry
(Chapter 13): partly to distance his followers' expectations of
the future from the worst excesses of apocalypticism, including
messianic pretensions (cf. 13.4–27), and partly to give qualified
credence to the notion of consummation contained in apocalyptic symbolism (13.24–7). At the heart of the presentation
stands a parable (the lesson of the fig-tree: 13.28), accompanied
by the exhortation to watchfulness (13.32–7); and these notes,
linked with some kind of allusion to the existential position of
'this generation' in relation to the Kingdom (cf. 13.30), may

well represent the general tenor of Jesus' use of apocalyptic imagery. The warning against messianic claims (cf. 'I am he' (13.6) – the very thing Jesus did not say at Caesarea Philippi: cf. 13.21f.) is linked directly with the Kingdom.[81] Apocalyptic language about the Kingdom frequently occurs in the context of misleading and fanatical claims, which can be linked to participation in the eschatological war to end all wars. Instead, Jesus emphasizes the accessibility of the Kingdom and, in spite of occasional use of dramatic images, substantially modifies even the language of apocalyptic, not to mention its world-view.

There is no space here to enter into yet another minefield of New Testament scholarship, viz., the 'son of man' debate. The phrase is used in the context of apocalyptic expectation in Mark 13.26 and appears secondary: i.e., Christian material adapted from Judaic apocalypticism. In Mark 14.62, however, Jesus seems to identify more immediately with the apocalyptic imagery. Under severe pressure, he accepts the damning title of Messiah and appears to link his present predicament with the future apocalyptic dénouement, expressed in essentially Danielic imagery. There is a number of less direct references to the divine tribunal in which the 'son of man' acts on behalf of the faithful (e.g. Luke 12.8) or executes divine judgement (e.g. Mark 8.38 par.). The most straightforward way to interpret such passages is to accede to the possibility that Jesus made free parabolic use of the Danielic images in particular to indicate the *telos* of his own ministry and of God's work. This would be entirely in character with his sensitivity to imagery and the tendency of his ministry: it would also considerably extend our concept of 'the parables of the Kingdom'. To this extent, but perhaps no further, the position suggested here has something in common with that of A. J. B. Higgins.[82] Otherwise, the phrase 'son of man' on Jesus' lips in the Gospels may be a Greek rendering of an Aramaic periphrasis (*bar nasha*) for the first person singular (Vermes) or, less probably, the Hebrew *ben adam* as a self-designation (Leivestad); a *mashal* or riddle saying in which Jesus is again proceeding parabolically (Black); or, on a mediating view, a blend of self-designation with messianic or quasi-messianic indications of Jesus' vocation and destiny (Lindars).[83] All that need be observed here is that 'son of man' phrases derive their meaning entirely from the sentence or context in which they occur.

Jesus was set on collision course with the religious establishment in Jerusalem: that is the clear import of the 'passion predictions' (Mark 8.31; 9.31; 10.33). If we were to press the question that the disciples were afraid to ask (9.32), viz., Why should Jesus' ministry necessarily take this direction?, any satisfactory answer would relate to his parabolic ministry of the Kingdom and its values. And this is precisely what Mark allows to emerge in his narrative. Jesus' course expresses, historically and experientially, the reversal of worldly values and the life-style of service (9.35); it is obedient to the vision of God the creator, rather than accommodating to 'hardness of heart' (10.5f.); and it involves receiving the yoke of the Kingdom in childlike fashion (10.15) and sacrificing even the last vestige of human reliance on the worldly support-systems (10.21f.; 13.31). It is a matter of acquiring clear vision (cf. 8.25) and following Jesus' way with faith-perception (10.52). It is his opponents who are blind. Thus Jesus comes to Jerusalem where his entry is taken, at least by his followers, to symbolize the coming Davidic kingdom (11.10); but the symbolism quickly becomes judgemental in the parabolic cursing of the fig tree (11.13f., 20)[84] and the purging of the temple (11.15ff.). The 'chief priests, scribes and elders' represent the opposition, arguing over authority or accreditation (always difficult in the prophetic tradition, 11.27–33) and unaware that the vineyard will be given to others (cf. 12.9; a parabolic reinterpretation of Isa. 5.1–7). The positive side of the Kingdom emerges in the controversies. The ambivalence of one's duty to the state emerges clearly in the dialectic (12.13–17): what truly belongs to God – the Kingdom? The resurrection controversy with the Sadducees serves to affirm that the Kingdom is not simply of this world (cf. 12.26f.). Scribes are not excluded by virtue of their professional class or by stereotype. One of them, affirming the inseparability of response to God and neighbour and refusing to allow the former to be reduced to temple-cult performance, is told, 'You are not far from the Kingdom of God'. The widow's mite symbolizes the total self-giving of Jesus' life-style (12.41–4, cf. 14.8). The repeated motif, however, is that the collision of this life-style with that of Israel's institutionalized practice occasions offence, alienation and hostility. But this factor was always present in parabolic discourse: it is not that Jesus' ministry has taken a different turn, inconsistent with earlier phases. It is rather that the parabolic method is pressed home by his actual presence in the institutionalized capital and so worked out in flesh and blood.

This is the precise context of the Last Supper (Mark 14.22–4 par.). The ostensible context is the Passover, with its evocative symbolism of God's kingly work for the salvation of his people; but regular liturgical practice is overtaken by the immediate drama that is being enacted as the climax of Jesus' ministry. 'As they were eating...': the familiarity of the act is part of its significance, recalling Jesus' practice of table-fellowship with his disciples – at times controversially extended to include others, so that the parabolic edge of the action collided with institutionalized convention (Mark 2.15ff. par.).[85] 'He took bread, and blessed, and broke it, and gave it to them...': the action recalls the heavy emphasis Mark placed on the feedings of the multitude, the riddle of Jesus' insistent discussion of bread and the disciples' failure to understand (cf. 8.14–21). There is a straight line in Mark's narrative between this prelude to Caesarea Philippi and the Last Supper, the eve of Jesus' death. Throughout his ministry he had warned his disciples against the 'leaven' of such as the Pharisees and Herod (8.15). Now positive identification is given to the 'bread' that Jesus has offered to them, as to the crowds, in such abundance (cf. 8.19f.): it is 'my body' – his self-giving, the giving of his very being. A cup, possibly one of four taken at the Passover, is made to underline the point that Jesus' self-giving – the giving of his life – is a covenantal renewal between God and his people (see Chapter four). This is Jesus' last act of table-fellowship 'until that day when I drink it new in the Kingdom of God' (Mark 14.25). The enactment of the fellowship of bread and wine is a parable of the Kingdom, 'a kind of appetizer (*antepast*) for the messianic banquet'.[86] In its performance, the participants share in the mystery of the reality which the parabolic act articulates and proclaims.

It is only in the final drama that Jesus' embodying of the Kingdom is made explicit. As already noted, he gives an unequi-

vocal answer – for the first time – to the question of his messiah-
ship, but immediately contextualizes it in apocalyptic imagery
(Mark 14.62). He gives only a marginally less direct answer to
the charge of being 'King of the Jews' (15.2), a title which runs
through the crucifixion narrative as a thread of the richest irony
(15.9, 12, 18, 26, 32). Thus the cross itself becomes a supreme
parable of the Kingdom, encapsulating in full measure the sum
total of the alienation involved in Jesus' parabolic ministry and
also the challenge to discern its affirmative statement (cf. 15.39).
Two related images interpret its meaning. One is a parable of
the temple, cited in evidence against Jesus (14.58; cf. Acts 6.14)
and pointing towards renewal or resurrection (cf. John 2.19ff.):
interestingly, Mark notes the shattering consequences of Jesus'
death for the temple (14.38; cf. Heb. 10.19f.). The other is the
resurrection image itself: not a parable of the Kingdom
(although the language used to express it is necessarily metaphorical or symbolic) but itself denoting one aspect of the
mystery of the Kingdom. Mark's account brings out something
of the paradox of resurrection faith. Jesus' remains had been
reverently laid to rest by Joseph of Arimathea, 'who was himself
looking for the Kingdom of God' (15.43); but the Kingdom
would not be found through the veneration of the holy relics, as
the women were to discover (16.1ff.). 'He has risen, he is not
here' (16.6): the resurrection registers the physical absence of
Jesus from the worldly scene:[87] he is not to be found in the
tomb. In the resurrection experiences, as in the eucharistic
presence, the encounter takes place within an apparent
absence.[88] On the other hand, 'He is going before you to Galilee'
(16.7; cf. 14.28): the promise is of dynamic leadership, the risen
Christ opening up their future way (in so far as they represent
the gist of what Jesus said, the 'passion predictions' can also be
interpreted in this way). The dynamic quality is readily illustrated from the 'signs of the Kingdom' in the ministry itself:
the *exousia* which healed the sick, raised the dead and brought
shalom. Luke's account tends to emphasize eucharistic presence
(24.30f.): the mystery of the eucharistic enactment is illumined
by the dynamic presence of the risen Christ, made known in the
moment of recognition. Matthew's narrative concludes with the
risen Christ on the mountain in Galilee, now possessed of 'all
exousia in heaven and on earth' (28.18), commissioning the

Church's mission in the threefold Name, and giving assurance of his eternal presence (28.19f.). Jesus the parabler, crucified and risen, is King, and his story is now the parable that must be told. Needless to say, it will be told in christological terms.

NOTES

1   As discussed in Chapter 1 above.
2   E. Schillebeeckx (1983), p. 143.
3   ibid.
4   Mackey (1979), pp. 127f.
5   cf. Perrin (1976), pp. 16f.
6   cf. Gibson (1981), pp. 77–82, esp. pp. 80f., where he describes the Hebrew notion of man as the viceroy of God.
7   Ps. 96.10 NEB. Perrin, op. cit., pp. 17f. prefers to translate 'Yahweh has become king!', thus emphasizing 'cultic avowal'. For 'enthronement' psalms, see Psalms 47, 93 and 96—99.
8   cf. Gray (1979); Whitelam (1979); Becker (1980).
9   Buber (1967), p. 139.
10 cf. von Rad (1962); Wright (1952); Smart (1979).
11 cf. Buber, op. cit., p. 162.
12 cf. Bright (1962), p. 203.
13 Ps. 2.7 and the 'royal' psalms generally.
14 cf. Johnson (1967).
15 Bright, op. cit., p. 204.
16 cf. Clements (1975), pp. 52ff.
17 Isa. 9.2–7; 11.1; cf. Zech. 9.9f.; 12.1—13.6.
18 Isa. 44.24—45.7; cf. 41.25f.; 46.8–11.
19 'A figure whose features are priestly and royal, but especially prophetic': Bright, op. cit., p. 340; cf. Isa. 42.1–4; 49.1–6; 50.4–9; 52.13—53.12.
20 de Jonge, NTS (1966), p. 140.
21 Vermes (1962), pp. 224, 227; cf. Vermes (1976), pp. 132f., 136, 198.
22 Vermes (1962), pp. 206f.
23 de Jonge, op. cit., p. 137.
24 Vermes (1976), p. 130.
25 Perrin (1976), p. 29.
26 Jerusalem Talmud, Ta'anith 68d.
27 Di Lella (1978), pp. 67–70.
28 ibid., p. 71.
29 Mackey (1979), p. 125.
30 For discussion of sources, cf. Colpe, TDNT 8, in loc.
31 Di Lella, op. cit., p. 87.
32 cf. Borsch (1967), pp. 139–43.
33 The imagery is biblical: cf. Hartman (1978), p. 217.
34 cf. Di Lella, op. cit., p. 94: his italics.
35 cf. The War Scroll, 1QM 1, tr. Vermes (1962), p. 125.

36 1QM 6.6; cf. 12.7, 19.
37 Allison (1985), p. 104.
38 Petuchowski (1968).
39 Dalman (1902), pp. 96–101; Vermes (1981), p. 22.
40 Gerhardssohn (1982), p. 30.
41 cf. Becker (1980).
42 Perrin (1976), p. 29.
43 Mackey (1979), p. 127.
44 cf. Josephus, *Ant.* XVIII. 116–19.
45 cf. Aune (1983), pp. 130ff.
46 cf. McDonald (1980), p. 17.
47 cf. Eisler (1931), p. 278; Dunn (1975), pp. 8ff.
48 cf. Aune, op. cit., p. 129.
49 cf. Wink (1968).
50 1QM; cf. Perrin (1976), p. 46.
51 cf. Cameron (1984), p. 246; Allison, op. cit., pp. 120–4.
52 cf. Chilton (1979), p. 229.
53 ibid., p. 230.
54 Via (1985), p. 60.
55 Miller (1981), pp. 125f.
56 Sanders (1985), pp. 106–13.
57 Perrin (1974), pp. 288–91; (1976), pp. 42f.
58 *contra* Kelber (1983), p. 117.
59 cf. Derrida (1980), pp. 158f.
60 i.e., derived from the 'history of religion' school.
61 Mackey (1979), p. 130.
62 So Kermode (1979), p. 31.
63 cf. Cranfield (1959), pp. 155f.
64 cf. Manson (1935), pp. 76–80; Chilton, *Rabbi* (1984), pp. 90–8.
65 cf. Chilton, ibid., p. 91.
66 cf. Kermode (1979), p. 30.
67 cf. Kelber (1976), pp. 47–60.
68 cf. Tannehill (1980), p. 84.
69 Kelber (1983), p. 75.
70 Perrin (1976).
71 (1936): cf. the title of his influential book.
72 Breech (1978), p. 38.
73 cf. Perrin (1976), p. 55.
74 Dodd (1936), p. 16.
75 Breech, op. cit., p. 35.
76 Kelber (1983), p. 64.
77 cf. Crossan (1975), pp. 63ff.
78 Mackey, op. cit., p. 134.
79 A major expression of the Kingdom – yet to be distinguished from the source of the Kingdom tradition in creation theology (see cameo i above) and in covenant discourse (see cameo ii above). It is clear that Jesus finds the source of Kingdom language in these more fundamental levels.
80 cf. the discussion in Chapter two, above.

81   cf. especially Luke 17.20f.; Perrin (1967), pp. 68–74; (1976), pp. 43f.
82   cf. Higgins (1980).
83   The works referred to are Vermes (1973); Leivestad (1968); Black (1947–8); and Lindars (1983).
84   cf. Telford (1980).
85   cf. Perrin (1967), p. 102.
86   Forrester, McDonald, Tellini (1983), p. 113; cf. Wainwright, (1978).
87   cf. Kelber (1983).
88   cf. Martelet (1976), p. 178.

4

The Praxis of the Kingdom

The Kingdom of God intersects the course of human history and experience. It is realized *par excellence* not in the dream world of apocalyptic nor in temple cult, legalistic casuistry, ascetic discipline nor power politics, but in personal and community life that is responsive to the call of God. Such intersection promotes a distinctive way of life that has a transcendent horizon and a faith-dynamic. This is what is denoted here by the term 'praxis', which has been described as 'the critical relationship between theory and practice whereby each is dialectically influenced and transformed by the other'.[1] For 'theory', read the faith-perception of a different order of reality from that which obtains in this alienated cosmos: viz., the new power denoted by the term 'Kingdom of God'. As the Kingdom presses upon this disordered cosmos, the new unrealized order enters into a dialectical relationship with the old, summoning all to become 'sensitized' to the demand of the complete or perfect order (cf. Matt. 5.48) and to express this sensitivity in praxis. There is thus a double 'sensitivity': to the dynamic, transcendent Kingdom and to the empirical situation: in short, to God and neighbour.

The mechanics of handling such a pervasive theme as the praxis of the Kingdom in the Gospels are daunting. However, the interaction of the Kingdom and historical experience assumes certain distinctive contours, which are sketched in this chapter. First, there is the question of initial summons, approach and encounter: 'entering the Kingdom', as the Evangelists put it. In this connection, the '*paidion* (child, boy) *pericopae*' are of immediate moment. Life within the Kingdom – the living

performance issuing from the interaction of transcendent Kingdom and historical existence – suggests liberation and obedience
as the twin motifs of discipleship; inherent in their juxtaposition
is the problem of the relationship between theonomy and the
autonomy of the human agent. These matters are discussed in
the second section of this chapter. Community is an important
aspect of life within the Kingdom. The 'dynamics of transcendence' operate in terms of the indivisible claim of 'the
other' upon us – God and neighbour; response to that claim sets
us in community with others. Striking expressions of that kind
of community are found in the group of disciples around Jesus.
Finally, there is the inevitability of conflict, arising from the
intersection of the Kingdom which 'is not of this world' with
the kingdom which is. The thematic structure of this chapter,
however, is not designed to obviate the problems of gospel
tradition and biblical interpretation, for the praxis of the Kingdom demands that account is taken of the ancient contexts in
which the traditions operated as well as those in which the
modern readers live and move and have their being.

1 ENTRY TO THE KINGDOM: THE '*PAIDION PERICOPAE*'

The summons to repentance is a classic prophetic form used by
John the Baptist and, apparently, by Jesus. Matthew, indeed,
ascribes the same utterance to both: 'Repent, for the kingdom
of heaven is at hand' (3.2; 4.17). Such a summons to repentance
can therefore hardly be said to be distinctive of Jesus. The
Evangelists, in fact, tend to present this aspect of his ministry in
secondary or summary terms. Mark's 'repent and believe in the
gospel' (1.15) belongs in form to Mark's own era rather than to
Jesus' ministry: there seems to be a deliberate blurring of the
distinction between them, in order to show the essential con-
tinuity between Jesus' message and that of early Christian
preachers (cf. Acts 2.38). There may be another reason. Even if
Jesus regularly employed the Hebrew notion *shub* ('turn back'
or 'repent'), his characteristic expression of it was clothed in
concrete and evocative imagery in the context of 'entering the
Kingdom' or life within the Kingdom. A typical example is

found in the complex '*paidion* ('child') *pericopae*' – their complexities indicating, perhaps, how heavily used they were in the early Christian communities as criteria of basic orientation and praxis.[2]

(i) THE 'PAIDION IN THE MIDST' PERICOPE (Mark 9.33–7 RSV)

Matt. 18.1–5	*Mark 9.33–37*	*Luke 9.46–48*
	33 And they came to Capernaum; and when he was in the house he asked them, "What were you discussing on the way?" [34] But they were silent; for on the way they had discussed with one another who was the greatest. [35]And he sat down and called the twelve; and he said to them, "If any one would be first, he must be last of all and servant of all." [36]And he took a child, and put him in the midst of them; and taking him in his arms, he said to them,	
1 At that time the disciples came to Jesus, saying, "Who is greatest in the kingdom of heaven?"		46 And an argument arose among them as to which of them was the greatest. [47]But when Jesus perceived the thought of their hearts,
		see Luke 9.48b
[2]And calling to him a child, he put him in the midst of them, [3] and said,		he took a child and put him by his side, [48]and said to them,
"Truly, I say to you, unless you turn and become like children, you will never enter the kingdom of heaven. [4]Whoever humbles himself like this child, he is the greatest in the kingdom of heaven.	see Mark 10.15	see Luke 18.17
5 "Whoever receives one such child in my name receives me."	9:37 "Whoever receives one such child in my name receives me; and whoever receives me, receives not me but him who sent me." see Mark 9:35b	9:48 "Whoever receives this child in my name receives me, and whoever receives me receives him who sent me; for he who is least among you all is the one who is great."

In this first major tradition, the complexities of the evidence defy any simple analysis in terms of source or form criticism. In Mark, verse 35 fits awkwardly into the context and its position betrays the hand of a redactor who has introduced it in order to respond to the context of the dispute about greatness (v. 34). Mark thus gives an interpretative lead into the pericope: viz., the truly pre-eminent are those who are counted last of all (or 'least', Luke 9.48b) on a worldly reckoning and who are distinguished by their willingness to serve all. The focus to which this interpretation relates is Jesus' placing of the *paidion* in the midst: a modelling or exemplification device which by its very nature is polyvalent. The particular line developed by the accompanying *logion* suggests that one's attitude to such *paidia* is a test of discipleship. One must 'receive' such a *paidion* as if he were Jesus himself: the typically polyvalent language suggests welcome, acceptance and the readiness to serve as appropriate responses. Jesus identifies with those of lowest status: to serve them is to serve him.

The polyvalence of the model, however, is reflected in the tension between the motifs extracted from it. Mark describes Jesus as taking the *paidion* in his arms, as in the act of blessing (cf. 10.16). This adds complexity to the narrative, for it is a different kind of action from setting the child in the midst, and the accompanying *logion* does not follow directly upon either. Baldly stated, the puzzle is as follows. The setting of the *paidion* in the midst suggests a model or example: *in some sense* (cf. v. 35), we should be 'as this *paidion*' (and not as we are, embracing false values). Jesus' act of taking the *paidion* in his arms suggests blessing: Jesus receives (blesses) the *paidion*: therefore, we should receive (bless, accept) all such *paidia* as he did. The final *logion* emphasizes Jesus' identification with such *paidia*: to 'receive' one such *paidion* is to receive Jesus, and to receive Jesus is to receive God.

But is there a puzzle about the meaning of *paidion*? M. Black[3] pointed to the fact that both 'servant' (*diakonos*, 9.33b) and '*paidion*' (9.36a) translate the Aramaic *talya*, which has the double meaning of 'servant' and 'boy'. The '*paidion* in the midst' episode therefore centres upon a dramatized play on the word *talya* in recognizably prophetic fashion (cf. Jer. 1.11; Amos 8.2). Apart from the light such a suggestion throws on Mark 10.15 (as discussed below), the *double entendre* goes far to elucidate the connection between the *paidion* as model and the *logion* on being 'last of all and servant of all' (9.35b). The logic is: model yourselves on this serving boy: Jesus himself is a servant of all and identifies with all servants: identifying similarly with all who serve, you must treat them as you would him: thus you will receive his blessing – indeed, God's blessing. At this point, the tradition coalesces with a whole range of material on the themes of identification with Jesus and of humility and service.

By contrast, Luke's narrative (9.46ff.), interpreting Jesus' intent as being 'to turn away the disciples' minds from thoughts of ambition to thoughts of ministry',[4] could be described as an intelligent reworking of Mark. Matthew, on the other hand, elucidates the meaning of the tradition by juxtaposing the general with the particular throughout the pericope (18.1–5). The overriding theme is, explicitly, the Kingdom of heaven (cf. 18.1, 3, 4), and the immediate context the question of greatness or pre-eminence within it (18.1). One particular *paidion* is set in the midst as model (18.2); a generalized implication is drawn in 18.3: we must 'turn and become like *paidia*' as the condition of entry to the Kingdom (see below). In 18.4 the narrative returns to the particular in a *logion* which seems to have been derived from the 'Q' tradition: 'whoever will humble himself like this *paidion*…' (cf. Matt. 23.12; Luke 14.11; 18.4): the *logion* directly elucidates the '*paidion* as model' theme. Finally, the generalizing tendency recurs in 18.5: to receive one such *paidion* is to receive Jesus; Matthew therefore concludes, like Mark, with the acceptance/identification motif. Thus Matthew presents a skilful version which interrelates the major nuances of the tradition. The main thrust is that, in place of seeking power and status, the Kingdom requires that we humble ourselves, shedding our self-importance and worldly values, and find our true vocation in obedient service to God as king: in doing so, we are one with Jesus and find him as we respect and bless the humble and lowly. It is worth observing that the emphasis in every part of this pericope is on people rather than on ideas, on action-in-the-world rather than on religious detachment from it (as distinct from its false values).

(ii) THE 'BLESSING OF THE PAIDIA' PERICOPE (Mark 10.13–16 par. RSV)

Matt. 19.13–15	*Mark 10.13–16*	*Luke 18.15–17*
13 Then children were brought to him that he might lay his hands on them and pray. The disciples rebuked the people; [14] but Jesus said,	13 And they were bringing children to him, that he might touch them; and the disciples rebuked them. [14] But when Jesus saw it he was indignant, and said to them,	15 Now they were bringing even infants to him that he might touch them; and when the disciples saw it they rebuked them. [16]But Jesus called them to him, saying,

Matt. 19.13–15	*Mark 10.13–16*	*Luke 18.15–17*
"Let the children come to me, and do not hinder them; for to such belongs the kingdom of heaven."	"Let the children come to me. do not hinder them; for to such belongs the kingdom of God.	"Let the children come to me, and do not hinder them; for to such belongs the kingdom of God.
See Matt. 18.3	[15]Truly, I say to you, whoever does not receive the kingdom of God like a child shall not enter it."	[17]Truly, I say to you, whoever does not receive the kingdom of God like a child shall not enter it."
15 And he laid his hands on them and went away.	[16]And he took them in his arms and blessed them, laying his hands upon them.	

For the form critics, the main feature of this pericope was taken to be the climactic saying or pronouncement of Jesus (Mark 10.14 par.: 'Let the *paidia* come to me...for to such belongs the Kingdom of God'). By contrast, the narrative element which supplies the setting or introduction may have been subject to a fair measure of editorial discretion. Luke's version corresponds most closely to this model, yet seems to be the most derivative and reductionist of the three. Luke treats the pericope simply as a double pronouncement story, in spite of the fact that he records the purpose of those bringing 'infants' (*brephē*) as being to obtain the touch of Jesus' hand: a feature which he fails to follow up. The second pronouncement (18.17) he appears to derive from Mark 10.15, which Matthew does not include in his version: we reserve this *logion* for discussion below. Matthew and Mark, on the other hand, give prominence at the beginning and the end of the pericope to Jesus' action in blessing: that is, the conveying of *shalom* by the holy man,[5] akin to healing in the broadest sense.[6] It is important, therefore, to note that the climax is an action and not simply a *logion* of Jesus (Best, 1981). For this reason, V. K. Robbins has described it in terms of rhetorical criticism, as a 'mixed chreia'.[7] It may be more meaningful to term it a symbolic action narrative which focuses directly on a distinctive and deliberate action of Jesus interpreted by the words he speaks and thrown into relief by the disciples' attitude which he rejects.

Reliance on an external model such as the 'chreia' of the rhetorical schools is not without its dangers. Robbins suggests that a combination of speech and action such as we have identified allows the character (*ethos*) of Jesus to emerge in a convincing way. Laying his hands on the children (explicit in

Matthew) is an action which 'manifests good character in Jesus that produces a strong favourable response (*pathos*)'.[8] Robbins' external model has led to non-contextual exegesis. Silberman is right in protesting at the modern perspective which is betrayed here, even if he overstates his case when he questions whether the narrative is directly concerned with a favourable response to Jesus[9] and suggests that 'it had nothing to do with kindness to children'. The issues are much deeper, for if the children symbolize the receptors of the Kingdom ('of such is the Kingdom of heaven'), then the blessing symbolizes the coming of the Kingdom as a gift. The gift is from God to the childlike; but the childlike themselves make a response: 'let them *come* to me' (hence the deep affinity of this pericope to the theme of 'entrance to the Kingdom'; cf. Mark 10.15 par.). The correlative to the blessing is the response of simple trust – as children respond to a loving parent, and as trust is engendered by loving acceptance. The *paidia* exemplify or typify those who know the reality of the reign of God, like 'the poor' and others in the beatitudes. The *logion* is close to the beatitude in form: 'blessed are the *paidia*, for of such (or 'theirs') is the Kingdom of heaven'. The disciples, as so often in Mark particularly, misread the situation and threaten to block or forestall the encounter of Jesus with the *paidia*. His command to them is direct: do not hinder!

(iii) INDEPENDENT 'ENTRANCE' SAYINGS

Matt. 18.3	*Mark 10.15*	*Luke 18.17*
Truly I say to you, unless you turn and become like children, you will never enter the kingdom of heaven.	[15]Truly, I say to you, whoever does not receive the kingdom of God like a child shall not enter it.	[17]Truly, I say to you, whoever does not receive the kingdom of God like a child shall not enter it. (RSV)

Matthew incorporates an entrance saying (18.3) in his '*paidion* in the midst' pericope, which is, as we have seen, a carefully edited composition. The *logion* in question interprets the focal symbol in relation to the issue of entering the Kingdom. The requirement is that we 'turn' or 'change course' by becoming 'like *paidia*'. The most obvious suggestion is that 'change and become...' is a rendering of the Semitic expression for 'repent',[10] denoting not so much the idea of regret for sins as a radical change of direction, a reorientation of one's life towards the Kingdom of God. To say that we must become 'like *paidia*' is to insist that no human achievement or merit, no human quality of 'greatness' brings one to the threshold of God's reign. The context in which Matthew places the *logion* suggests that an act of humility is in view (cf. 18.4). Humility is not normally predicated of a child in any literal sense, unless indeed the 'serving boy' connotation is presupposed. In that case, the meaning in Matthew is that one must change from one's ambitious quest for human status and learn the meaning of service: *that* involves a major act of humility on the part of the adult concerned. But the context is secondary and may be at variance with the basic denotation of the *logion*, viz., to shed all adult self-sufficiency and make a new beginning with God as king.

The other form of the tradition – Mark 10.15 = Luke 18.17 ('whoever does not receive the Kingdom as a *paidion*') – has its own difficulties.[11] Here we need focus only on what it means to receive the Kingdom of God 'as a *paidion*'. Is *paidion* subject or object? Attempts have been made from time to time[12] to take *paidion* as an accusative: to receive the Kingdom as one receives a child. Robbins[13] is the most recent advocate of this view. The maxim in Mark 10.15 is a comment on Jesus' receiving the children into his arms: 'Once the statement has been made that Jesus "received" the children into his arms, it would be natural to refer to "receiving" the Kingdom rather than "belonging" to it.' With respect, it would not be 'natural' at all: it would be incompetent for a redactor to behave in this way! If Mark 10.15 is redactional (as it probably is), its purpose is to expand the reader's understanding of the pericope in some important way – not to introduce a contradictory logic.

Sauer[14] and Tannehill[15] rightly point out that Mark 10.15 gives an important reason for associating the Kingdom with children; and Robbins himself comments that 'Jesus' receiving of the children presented an analogy for receiving the Kingdom'. It is important, however, to observe the basis on which the analogy works. Jesus' action in *blessing* the children is the symbol of the coming of the Kingdom to them (cf. 10.16). Their reception of the Kingdom is an active response: 'let them come to me...' Hence, the analogy of reception presupposes the *activity* of the *paidia*. All must receive the Kingdom as a *paidion* does: *paidion* is subject, not object. The *paidia* symbolize those to whom the Kingdom belongs: therefore, we must receive the Kingdom in similar fashion if we are to have any hope of entering it.

In such parabolic metaphor, Jesus gave performance to the Kingdom in a particularly trenchant way. The parable suggests that there is an immediate and all-important step which must be taken in order to enter the Kingdom *now*. In the parable, the Kingdom addresses us and calls for a response which is of primary significance for our life and destiny. In this sense, the Kingdom is powerfully actualized in Jesus' parabolic performance and in our responsive performance. Yet the Kingdom is far from exhaustively actualized. It stretches before us as God's future and ours: a future on which we have embarked and in which we presently share as we enter the Kingdom – like a *paidion*.

(*iv*) THE 'PAIDION' ARCHETYPE.   When Jesus insisted that, as the precondition of entry to the Kingdom, one must 'become as a *paidion*', he was appealing effectively to an archetypal symbol, a universal image or metaphor[16] that expresses a particular aspect of life-sense in depth. In Jungian psychology, in which attention is paid both to archetypes in general and to the child archetype in particular,[17] 'the child motif represents the pre-conscious, childhood aspect of the collective psyche'.[18] Theologically, it suggests that adults have to face the possibility that their present life-style is at variance with their fundamental humanity; i.e., they have become inauthentic, artificial, rootless. Jung wrote: 'All this presents a favourable opportunity for an equally vehement confrontation with the primary truth.'[19]

Sayings both in the '*paidia*' and the 'Kingdom' tradition frequently work towards this end. There is the need to jettison false values such as wealth, materialism, status-seeking, power – all of them indices of inauthentic being and barriers to entry to the Kingdom. This side of the equation emphasizes the cost: the abandonment of invalid securities, loss, death. One must learn to 'die', to 'bear the cross' – but in order to 'find life'. Hence, the *paidion* archetype is more than a dissociation from the past. As Jung puts it, 'The child is potential future';

'life is a flux, a flowing into the future, and not a stoppage or a backwash.'[20] The *paidion* archetype, subsuming the more usual model of repentance (Heb. *shub*), denotes more than a change of direction. It suggests new life and rebirth, as in the more explicit Johannine imagery (cf. John 3.3, 5). But how does Jesus come to use the language and imagery of the *paidia*? His use of this metaphor suggests a dependency neither on the more enlightened Hellenistic estimate of *paidia*[21] nor on a positive doctrine of the child in terms of its sinlessness or innocence (hints of which are found in Hellenistic Judaism: e.g., 2 Macc. 8.4, Philo, *Leg. Gai.* 234). Implicit in his use of the image is a comparison with adults: *paidia* are 'modest and unspoiled as compared with adults';[22] they are 'open to the fatherly love of God, whereas grown-ups so often block it'.[23] Hence, the striking statements Jesus makes or implies about *paidia* are essentially the product of his parabolic procedure, and as such they give dramatic expression to the call to adults to make a new beginning, to have a new responsiveness and openness to God and other people (especially 'those of low estate'), and so to learn or relearn the ways of God. In this sense, one may rediscover lost potential, integrity and wholeness.[24] And these developments take place not in the course of some isolated religious quest but in the context of the Kingdom of God which is *entos humon* ('in your midst'): the Kingdom into which we dare to move forward at Jesus' invitation ('all such developments and transactions are extraordinarily difficult and dangerous', Jung observed),[25] and where we find our own destiny gifted to us in the dynamic relationship with God and neighbour.

At this point, the '*paidion*' archetype in the Gospels transcends the limits of the 'child' archetype and shades into the connotation of the servant. Are we then to speak also of the 'servant' archetype? The 'Servant Songs' of Isaiah might impel us in that direction: it is through the brokenness of the servant that Israel is redeemed and light is brought to the Gentiles. A similar quality is evinced in the ministry of Jesus (not least in the 'son of man' sayings), while the pre-Pauline tradition of Phil. 2.5-11 places the 'servant' image at the centre of God's dealings with mankind in Christ. Appeal is made to the 'servant' symbol partly because it expresses the antithesis of power, status and domination – the destructive drives; and partly because it suggests realization of human potentiality through acceptance of others and the building of community. It operates through a model of self-giving (cf. 'he emptied himself'): not as exaggerated self-deprecation but as reaching out to others in neighbour-love. Here is the dynamic of the new creation, representing the outworking and therefore the essential complement to the 'child' symbol: it is a uniting, even redemptive, symbol, turning the loss of 'dying' into the gain of life renewed. Hence, the motifs of 'child' and 'servant' are not two distinct archetypes in New Testament usage but rather coalesce in the archetypal *paidion*.

One special feature of the *paidion* archetype should be mentioned. It is not the stuff of dreams; it is rooted in and related to historical praxis. As Hans-Ruedi Weber has properly observed, 'Jesus had a fully realistic view of children'.[26] He did not idealize them nor speak of them in a sentimental way, as the parable of the children's game clearly shows.[27] But there is a constant interplay in the *paidion* tradition between the historically specific and the symbolic. The former is exemplified in the blessing of the children; the latter predominates in the *paidion* in the midst pericope. The former tradition, which is so clearly concerned with actual children, includes the *logion*, 'for to such belongs the Kingdom of God' (Mark 10.14c): a clear move from the specific to the symbolic. Conversely, the *paidion* in the midst, though basically a model for adults to emulate and therefore symbolic, does not rule out Jesus' acceptance of a particular servant-boy: indeed, the lesson developed through the complexity of the tradition is that disciples of Jesus must show similar acceptance to those of humble status. There is no good ground for assuming that generalizing comments such as Mark 10.14c are necessarily secondary:[28] the evidence suggests that such an interpretation was characteristic of Jesus. Not only does Jesus move from the historical to the symbolic in his teaching, but the symbolic opens out on historical praxis. To encounter the *paidion* archetype in gospel tradition is to be motivated towards a life of service. It is this historical emphasis above all which differentiates authentic traditions of Jesus' teaching from gnostic speculations.[29]

2 LIBERATION AND OBEDIENCE

The immediate consequence of encountering the Kingdom is the paradoxical combination of liberation and obedience. The context in which their interaction is developed is the community of disciples gathered round Jesus, himself the enactor of the Kingdom.

(i) LIBERATION   According to the Marcan presentation, Jesus' enactment of the Kingdom in word and deed evoked surprise and astonishment (Mark 1.22 par.; 2.12 par.), for it was characterized by *exousia*, the power of the Spirit effective in changing the lot of those in bondage to alien powers (Mark 1.27; cf. 3.28ff.). In Luke, this liberation motif is expounded with particular force (cf. 4.18f.). Jesus' proclamation and ministry signal the time of fulfilment (4.21): the time when Scripture is fulfilled, the Kingdom actualized, and people summoned to final decision;[30] and when welcome news is given to the poor, release to the captives, sight to the blind and freedom to the oppressed. Couched in LXX terms, Luke's programmatic formula[31] indicates a particular constituency to whom the Kingdom brings liberation: a disadvantaged and disabled group extending beyond the frontiers of Israel (cf. 4.25–30). Like the exorcized demoniacs, all such were in a position to recognize the dynamic power of the Kingdom that had transformed their situation by a veritable act of God (Luke 11.20) or access to his Spirit (Matt. 12.28).

If this liberating programme is summed up as 'good news for the poor' (Luke 4.18; Isa. 61.1), in what sense is the term 'poor' used? Evidence of Luke's 'material crudeness'[32] is seen in his version of the beatitude: 'Blessed are you poor...' (Luke 6.20, 24); but if 'poor' denotes a socio-economic group, then the blessedness can refer only to their liberation from the hopelessness and despair of poverty. There is nothing attractive or creative about poverty and deprivation. Indeed, there are indications in Luke and his sources (L and Q) of a hostility to wealth (cf. 16.19–31) and a reversal of fortunes in favour of the poor (1.53) which may reflect the economic conditions endured by Palestinian Christians from the time of the acute famine in Claudius' reign (AD 41–54) until the Jewish revolt.[33] The Old

Testament tradition, however, testifies not only to the divine concern for the poor shown by Yahweh, the Liberator (cf. Exod. 20.1; Deut. 5.6) and the corresponding concern that must be shown by his people Israel for the economically oppressed (e.g., Deut. 5.14; 14.29; 15.1ff., 7, 12ff.; 24.19, 22); but also to 'the poor' ('anāwîm) as a 'reversal' term for those close to Yahweh. It is used in this way in the devotional theology of the Psalms (e.g., Ps. 40.17; 70.5), in intertestamental literature (e.g. Psalms of Solomon) and at Qumran.[34] Hence in Matthew, the Kingdom is given not simply to the poor but to 'the poor in spirit',[35] admittedly a polyvalent term, but one which relates to the Jewish devotional tradition; just as 'the hungry' (Luke 6.21a) are specifically those who hunger and thirst after 'the righteousness' (i.e., the Kingdom: Matt. 5.6).

The essential feature is that they are ready and eager for the transformation which the Kingdom entails and which is already making its demands on them. Hence the Sermon on the Mount – of which Matthew rather than Jesus should, strictly speaking, be regarded as author[36] – presupposes a disciple group (cf. 'brother' in 5.22ff.) whose way of life is characterized by 'anāwîm piety in the context of the Kingdom. In fact, there is multiple attestation for this itinerant disciple-group who had left all to follow Jesus. It is characterized by joy at the enactment of the Kingdom in its midst, and in the spontaneity and totality of its response. Its way of life can thus be described in terms of the voluntary surrender of worldly ties and possessions, gentleness of bearing and non-militancy in relations with others: thus it looked to the consolation of the Kingdom, its God-given inheritance. Hence the term 'poor', like the term *paidia*, represents a primary focus of meaning, an archetypal symbol of the praxis of the Kingdom. It set the pattern for the itinerant Christian apostles who succeeded the disciples and for the community of goods and charitable ministries in the early Church. But it also set a pattern for believers who were not themselves called to this degree of discipleship. Faced with the demand of the Kingdom, all must learn to distance themselves from the false security of wealth, the brutalizing quest of power and the distracting preoccupation with worldly care, even when it is accepted that worldly concerns continue to have a certain practical importance (cf. Matt. 6.32f.). Through the response of faith to the approach of the Kingdom, one is given a new set of priorities, a new perspective on life which embraces the liberation that God offers. But this liberation is not only liberation *from* destructive preoccupations, it is also liberation *for* discipleship, whether in its thorough-going form (i.e., as the twelve and their close associates) or in some wider faith-pattern. And liberation for discipleship implies the new obedience which life in the Kingdom necessarily entails.

(ii) THE TWIN COMMANDMENT TO LOVE.   The focus of the new obedience is found in the twin commandment to love. Its centrality is illustrated by the introductory question in the various redactions of the tradition. In Mark, one of the scribes asks the straightforward question, 'Which commandment is first of all?' (Mark 12.28); in Matthew, a lawyer asks combatively, 'Which is the great commandment of the law?' (cf. Matt. 22.35f.); in Luke, the lawyer's question is made to relate directly to human destiny, 'What shall I do to inherit eternal life?' (Luke 10.25), thus leaving it for Jesus to make reference to the law (10.26). It is not adequate exegesis to dismiss such features as *merely* redactional: the redactions give important guides to interpretation. The debate is about supreme obligation as expressed in the law: which is tantamount to discussing the overriding priority for human life and destiny. Like the symbol of the Kingdom itself, the question of primary obligation derives from Scripture and, in a Jewish context, is to be settled in scriptural terms. There can be little doubt about Jesus' acceptance of the twin commandment as expressing the primary moral requirement of the law.[37]

The human response which is integral to the twin commandment also merits consideration. The Deuteronomic phrase 'with all thy heart and with all thy soul' suggests 'the devotion of the *whole* being to God':[38] 'heart' denoting the intellect in Hebrew psychology and 'soul' the desires or affections. Deut. 6.5 adds, 'with all thy might': i.e., with all the power that is yours to command, in terms of 'external resources, power, mammon'.[39] There is considerable difficulty in translating Hebrew anthropological terms into Greek: four terms are used, with a degree of tautology. The phrase 'with all your heart' (*kardia*) now means 'wholeheartedly': the response must not

be 'half-hearted' or partial, as in legalistic practice, facile
observance or hypocritical conduct. 'With all your soul' (*psuche*)
means that one's whole life, oneself, is to be given to God: as
in 'whoever loses his life (lit. *psuche*) for my sake (and the
gospel's) will save it' (Mark 8.35 par.). 'With all your mind'
(*dianoia*) suggests the cognitive realm but in the predominant
sense of 'understanding', 'perception' and 'insight' (*sunesis*).
While the cognitive is clearly important for Mark, it is unjustified
to find in his account 'a decidedly rationalistic aspect'.[40]
The weighting of 'mind'/'understanding' barely offsets the
emphasis on 'heart' and 'soul'. 'With all your strength' (*ischus*)
picks up the Hebrew notion of resources or power. In a negative
or half-hearted response to God, mammon – whether as wealth,
privilege or status – becomes a rival to God: 'no one can serve
two masters' (Matt. 6.24; Luke 16.13). It is important to note
that in the Marcan presentation, this total response to God
represents a quality of devotion which transcends even the cult
of Israel and is explicitly declared to be 'not far from the
Kingdom of God' (12.34): an example of litotes or understatement, as Furnish[41] rightly indicates. The scribe is un-
questionably within the Kingdom, and rightly identifies the
mainspring of its praxis. But what implications does this have
for 'the ethics of the Kingdom'?

(iii) THE ETHICS OF THE KINGDOM.   The debate about 'the
ethics of the Kingdom' has been made more problematic than
it need have been by the philosophical assumptions and
exegetical inadequacies of many of its participants. The first
problem arises from the language of command (or commandment). Some writers have proceeded as if such language could
only be interpreted literally as an order and thus, consciously or
otherwise, assume a command theory of ethics. Frequently,
they proceed without discussing the matter[42] or leave it inad-
equately clarified.[43] The language of command simply expresses
an imperative or conveys obligation: the context must be carefully explored in order to determine the precise nature of the
requirement. Left unclear, the first problem creates mischief for
the second, viz., how can love (*agape*) be commanded?[44] In
order to avoid the solecism that an emotion can be commanded,
some commentators have defined *agape* in such a way as to

underplay its emotional content. In some of his writings C. H. Dodd denied that *agape* was 'primarily an emotion or an affection', and insisted that it was 'primarily an active determination of the will':[45] a line of argument subsequently adopted by Fletcher.[46]

Various objections can be made at this point. Exegetically, the argument is particularly weak. The twin commandment clearly presupposes the response of 'the whole being'; and the Greek 'heart and soul', like the Hebrew 'soul', certainly does not exclude the emotions. Examples of love in the New Testament frequently suggest deep emotion, whether on the part of Jesus himself or in a parabolic context. Compassion may have a conative element but it is not without an affective connotation! Besides, it is extremely doubtful whether the Dodd–Fletcher line really meets the philosophical requirement. How much force are we to give to the adverb 'primarily'? If the emotions are secondary, what role do they actually play in *agape*? If they operate at all (as they must), does not this invalidate this particular attempt to show that love can be commanded?

A third problematic bequest of command language is the suggestion of a 'non-autonomous ethic' as the corollary of the twin commandment.[47] God is the source of the norms, both of faith and ethics: hence 'the non-autonomy of ethics' and 'the inconceivability of a non-ethical faith'. But non-autonomy is a confused and confusing term. It may be used, as it is by Via, to indicate that faith and ethics are internally related: since ethics is not independent of faith, it is non-autonomous. It could be used crudely to demonstrate that the ethics of the Kingdom derive from the king: subjects may not do what they like, for that would mean anarchy, licence or rebellion: hence, deontological (cf. *dei*: 'it is necessary'), non-autonomous ethics. But Via seems to recognize that this simple model is unsatisfactory and transposes his discourse into a relational, responsive key. 'Only if the disciple loves with the whole being the one God over all...can the disciple be enabled to have the freedom to love without reserve.'[48] Hence the great commandment – given in the context of the Shema, as Mark reminds his readers – belongs to the relational realm of discourse, within which motivation and inspiration are found.

One of the most helpful features of Mark's presentation

(12.28–34) is that the loving relationship to God and neighbour is shown to be integral to an understanding of the Kingdom of God (12.34). The Kingdom is presented by Mark as 'the good news of God' (1.14f.). In other words, one has so internalized the divine imperative that one begins to discover one's true autonomy in joyful obedience. And this means liberation, fulfilment. Divine obligation is encountered as heteronomous only by the 'hard of heart', who in their alienation from God cannot enter into the faith-context that makes love possible. Ultimately, the divine will is encountered by all such as judgement (cf. Matt. 25.41–6). But within the faith-context there is *theonomy* – the Kingdom of God; and those attuned to it may well fulfil the divine requirements without realizing that they do so (cf. Matt. 25.34–40). The paradox of the ethics of the Kingdom is that theonomy and human autonomy are not set in opposition to each other, as they are in the setting of alienation; rather, the one is the obverse of the other. Hence, in God's service we find our perfect freedom.

The ethics of the Kingdom represents an intrinsic part of the logic of the Kingdom itself. It presupposes the divine enactment of the Kingdom in the ministry of Jesus: hence, the narrative of the ministry must always be told as the witness to 'the good news of God'. Enactment and story, like parable, presuppose interaction and the dynamics of community life;[49] just as the twin commandment to love presupposes interdependent community as an expression or performance of the Kingdom. Hence *koinonia* is the essential catalyst for the working of the Kingdom *entos humon*: the *koinonia* that consists of and suggests the 'little ones', the poor in spirit and pure in heart who are not only promised the vision of God but who actively give performance to his Kingdom now. It is in this direction that the paradox of liberation and obedience finds resolution. The problem is not discerned in terms of philosophical abstraction: it is seen as integral to the paradox of life itself, which must be surrendered in order to be realized. It is finally resolved not in intellectual terms but in flesh and blood: in life-with-others, open to God and neighbour.

3 COMMUNITY AND SELF-GIVING

(i) THE FELLOWSHIP OF DISCIPLES.   The fellowship of disciples
rested on the fact that all its members had received a call[50] or
commission[51] which entailed leaving their former way of life and
mode of subsistence.[52] The general commission, expressed in
the metaphor of fishing, was made more specific by the
commissioning of the twelve to extend Jesus' own 'ministry of
the Kingdom' (Mark 3.13–19 par.; Mark 6.7–13 par.; cf. Matt.
9.35). They learned from him how to pray: in particular,
the prayers of the Kingdom (cf. Matt. 6.10; Luke 11.2), of
obedience to the King whom one can nevertheless address as
abba, Father (Mark 14.36 par.).[53] They had to model their
mission on him: receiving his words when they were with him,
and imitating his actions. Their role was therefore mimetic;[54]
they safeguarded the tradition and praxis of the Kingdom as
they transmitted it.

The dynamics of this group were exceedingly complex.
Characteristically but not invariably, it was an open group.
After Levi's commission, it encompassed 'tax collectors and
sinners' within its table fellowship (Mark 2.15 par.). That particular kind of act or performance, totally ignoring the strictly
drawn conventions of religiosity, represented a theme of Jesus'
ministry which became an issue in society. Part of the offence
was the joyous freedom of Jesus' table practice: '...the son of
man came eating and drinking, and they say, "Behold, a glutton
and drunkard, a friend of tax collectors and sinners!"' (Matt.
11.19; cf. Luke 7.34f.). The disciples' fellowship was joyous and
spontaneous, like a marriage celebration, and characterized by a
sense of a new order of things that demanded new forms of
expression. But if the new age was experienced, however pro-
leptically, as a reality in their midst, the old age struck back. The
bridegroom will not be with them for ever (cf. Mark 2.20). The
crux is the offence which the new radical order, the performance
of the Kingdom in the midst, gave to the synthetic conventionality of the existing guardians of faith. The safe marker-
buoys were removed; the necessary separation of the holy and
the unclean, the righteous and the sinners, 'us and them', was
deliberately undermined, for the dynamic of the Kingdom did
not respect such parameters but set before all, equally, the need

for repentance and healing. Sometimes it is suggested that the Gospels are anachronistic and grossly unfair to the Pharisaic tradition in particular. This, however, is to miss the point. The Pharisees and related groups typify the religious opposition to the dynamic of the Kingdom in the given cultural context, just as the Herodians typify the political opposition. But the identification of such opposition does not limit the offence of Jesus' praxis to ancient Judaism alone: it presents no less a challenge to Christian groups today. Perrin is wholly justified in describing Jesus' table fellowship as an acted parable[55] but only partly justified in suggesting that 'a regular table fellowship, in the name of the Kingdom of God, between Jesus and his followers, when these followers included "Jews who had made themselves Gentiles"'[56] was the decisive factor in bringing about the death of Jesus (cf. Mark 3.6 par.). The theological theme adopted by Jesus here was not unparalleled among the teachers of Judaism, although it can rarely if ever have received the positive enactment given it by the disciples' table fellowship, which may well have been a recurring focus of offence. Other historical factors, such as the challenge to the temple, may have been of more immediate effect in the particular chain of events leading to the crucifixion. But in so far as the table fellowship was parabolic, it encapsulated that tendency to disconcert and disorientate, even to dislocate one's view of the world and hence to alienate, that is part of the cutting edge of parabolic engagement.

Jesus' family or clan was seen to be disconcerted in precisely this way. When his family group would have claimed him with a kind of proprietorial or protective air, Jesus distinguished the priority of the disciple group – those sitting about him – from that of the clan. The bond of disciple-fellowship was the dynamic of the Kingdom – doing the will of God (Mark 3.35). Jesus too had 'left everything', including his family, to respond to his commission. Hence, blood relatives were 'outsiders', just as the scribes were.[57] The precondition of all such dialogue, however, was the openness of the group to the world. Sometimes the pressure from outside was so great that it was impossible to have a meal at all (Mark 3.20). The vulnerability of the group was a given factor in its life-style.

Sometimes, however, the disciple-fellowship was a more

intimate, 'inside' group, although it often appears to be somewhat larger than the twelve (cf. Mark 4.10). This was the mimetic
group, appointed to 'be with' Jesus (Mark 3.14) and shaped by
his teaching and praxis. To it was given the mystery of the
Kingdom (Mark 4.11 par.); to it everything was explained
(Mark 4.34). Over against it were the uncomprehending crowds,
rendered outsiders by parabolic riddles to which they had no
key, and by their own 'hardheartedness'. Yet the dynamics of
the disciple-fellowship were affected by the way parables
worked within the group. The disciples shared the incompre-
hension of the crowds: they did not understand the parable of
the sower. It was one thing to proclaim repentance and the
imminence of the Kingdom, even to be its instrument in
exorcism and healing: but what was this talk of a Kingdom in
process now, disappointed in much of its attempted growth, yet,
indiscernibly and independently of human action, bringing its
own abundant harvest? Thorough-going eschatology is straightforward; parabolic explorations make life difficult. And this
is typical of parabolic dynamics, viz., to effect a reversal of
expectation[58] and to 'alienate' the hearers so that they too experience the 'outsider' role. There is, of course, always the possibility (open to the crowds also) of changing course (cf. 4.12c)
and genuinely opening oneself to the mystery of the Kingdom.
Hence the disciple-group was characterized by paradox. Privi-
leged, close to Jesus, taught by him and commissioned to the
work of the Kingdom, it could enter further into the Kingdom
it served only by becoming totally disconcerted about it. This
process of alienation might come about through puzzlement
at the parables or through their own wrong choices (cf. Mark
10.35-44). It was never enough to plead that they had left everything and followed Jesus (Mark 10.28). That they had done so
would bring its own rewards; but they were under the constant
obligation to receive the Kingdom 'like a child' (10.15). Hence
disequilibrium is an essential part of growth and development as
children of the Kingdom (cf. Mark 10.24).

Yet the disciple-fellowship was in itself an important com-
ponent of Jesus' ministry. In spite of all its tensions – one notes
that from the narrative of the call of the twelve onwards Judas
is designated as traitor (Mark 3.19 par.) – its very existence and
its openness to the outside world represented a particular ex-

pression or performance of the Kingdom (cf. Matt. 8.11; Luke 13.29). It is not strange that the consummated Kingdom is imaged in the messianic feast, of which the extended table fellowship of the disciple-group was a concrete performance. And just as 'neighbour' could become a focus of alienation in parable, so a truly open *koinonia* was offensive in its ritual presentation of 'an experience of God as the father who cherished all and graced all equally, and in this way inspired all to cherish and grace each other'.[59]

(ii) FELLOWSHIP SYMBOLS AND RITUAL   Jesus' table fellowship with his disciples had its own ritual, and when the fellowship was extended to embrace the crowds in their thousands the eucharistic nature of the ritual became evident: taking the elements, invoking heaven, blessing, breaking and giving; the disciples serving the people (cf. Mark 6.41 par.). In the apparently duplicate tradition in Mark 8.1–10 and Matt. 5.32–9, the emphasis on the ritual action is as strong as ever: giving thanks (*eucharistēsas*), blessing (*eulogēsas*), breaking, and giving...; and, as in the first story, the abundance of the gifts is underlined. In such ritual, what is being done reflects the nature of the community and also establishes and confirms it: it *effects* community. The disciple-community, however, not only comprises the fellowship of Jesus with his followers on the level of personal intimacy; it also embodies an element of transcendental awareness, of involvement in the mystery of the Kingdom through Jesus' ministry. Hence problems of meaning and praxis are inherent in the life of the group and in its liturgical experience. It is presumably for this reason that what is ostensibly a third treatment of the same theme is included in Mark 8.14–21 and Matt. 16.5–12. Here, the unacceptable response to the Kingdom that characterized Jesus' opponents (the Pharisees and Herod in Mark, the Pharisees and Sadducees in Matthew, the Pharisees in Luke) is imaged as their 'leaven', which works *in malam partem* and produces 'hardheartedness', 'obtuseness', 'failure to understand'.[60] At times, faced with awesome mystery, the disciples found themselves in an analogous position (Mark 8.17f.; cf. 4.10–13; 6.52). The dynamics of the disciple community, however, were designed to bring them through disorientation, doubt and confusion to discern the signs of the

Kingdom in their midst: not least in the breaking and sharing of bread and other food in ritual action. For Mark, at least, the giving of the loaves represented an encoded act of God that threw light on the whole ministry of Jesus. They had fed thousands, and there were many full baskets of fragments left over: bread for others not present (unlike the manna, which had to be eaten on the spot). Thus the bread they had in their midst was a mighty resource, which could strengthen them in their time of danger as it could feed multitudes. It represented in some way the present operation of the Kingdom in their midst, the gift of God for the strengthening of his people: and it was given by Jesus. Mark leaves us with the question Jesus put to the disciples: 'Do you not yet understand?'

The *hermeneusis* or interpretation of symbolic meaning receives fullest expression at the last supper. The passover meal was rich in symbolism: from the bitter herbs to the songs of liberation. During the meal Jesus took a piece of bread, the central symbol of their own fellowship. He performed the familiar ritual: the blessing, the breaking, the sharing; but now, for the first time, gave the parabolic *hermeneusis*: 'This is my body'. In that statement there was given clarification of the mystery which had exercised the minds of the disciples for so long. Throughout their association in the disciple-fellowship Jesus had given himself to them as he had broken bread with them; in the celebrations with the crowds, he had given himself to them, as he shared the bread and fish with them. Now, as he gave the bread and the cup (another evocative image, expressing identity of purpose) at what was avowedly his last supper, he gave himself to them finally as the hour of his death approached. Here is the gift of life: new life, life for the future. And here the self-giving of Jesus blends with the theme of resurrection, his and theirs. The image of the messianic feast in the last days can serve to denote reunion in glory (cf. Mark 14.25; Matt. 26.29; cf. Luke 22.18). But the power of the Kingdom is expressed not so much by such images of the eschaton as by the performance, the praxis, which the disciple community will give to it in the strength of Jesus' self-giving. The mystery of the Kingdom will be realized in the body to which Christ gives his life. In giving himself to his people Jesus is not thereby putting himself at their disposal: he is also transcendent, 'going before them' (cf. Mark 14.29; Matt. 26.32), leading them in the ways of God's Kingdom. Luke places the dispute about greatness immediately after his account of the Last Supper (22.24–30): its central theme being 'let the greatest among you become as the youngest, and the leader as one who serves' (Luke 22.26). John concurs in this theme: for John, the true parable of the Last Supper was the washing of the disciples' feet (John 13.1–20). Like all parables, the parable of the Last Supper is polyvalent; but the parable theme consistently coheres in the invitation and summons to life within the Kingdom of God.

4 THE KINGDOM AND THE KINGDOMS

Jesus' ministry, enacting the Kingdom of God, ends in the cross. Why? The answer is found in the peculiar paradox of the Kingdom. Its ethos is not the political or economic power which keeps others in a position of dependence: 'it shall not be so among you' (Mark 10.42f. par.). It is not expressed in the prestige and status of religious conventionality: Jesus taunts his religious critics with their love of ostentation and their rejection of the implications of true community. It is differentiated from unqualified eschatological expectation, which can be exploited for political, religious or selfish ends (cf. Mark 13.21; Matt. 24.23); the Kingdom of God is *entos humon* (Luke 17.21). And when Jesus says in the Fourth Gospel, 'My Kingdom is not of this world' (John 18.36), he expressly differentiates it from the kingdoms that rest on coercion or violence. But the paradox is that Jesus' enactment of this 'unworldly' Kingdom is of political significance in the world. If he moves within the horizons of transcendence, it is a worldly transcendence he expresses: one that can be enacted in the world, and that can express specific motifs and thematic possibilities. Its enactment is a challenge and rebuke to all worldly power-systems. Hence 'my Kingdom is not of this world' is a political statement, part of the dialogue that relates to a charge of treason brought against Jesus.

(i) LOVE TO ENEMY AS A STRATEGY OF THE KINGDOM. The command to love one's enemies[61] is not a simple extension of the command to love one's neighbour. It is much more than a general expression of goodwill towards humanity, more than the overcoming of selfish will, and more than a limited openness to one's enemy that might require some gestures of conciliation before the mechanisms of self-defence are brought into play. Matt. 5.44f. presupposes a social context: the faith-community is encountering opposition, even persecution in society. The horizons are transcendental, as always in Kingdom discourse: you shall act as children of your heavenly Father (Matt. 5.45), you must be *teleioi* ('complete', 5.48). Though members of a group, you must not react with an absence of love ('hate') towards those whose group loyalties and interests are divergent or opposed. At Qumran, for example, group solidarity was fierce (cf. 1QS 1.10, 9.20), while clan solidarity is a phenomenon common to many cultures. The group dynamics prompted by the Kingdom are very different: characterized, as we have seen, not by exclusiveness or defensiveness but by an openness to others that, indeed, reflects the openness of God to his children. Hence, one must take issue at this point with Luise Schottroff when she claims, in the course of an excellent discussion, that love to enemies 'is not interested in what goes on in the heart of the one who loves'.[62] The emphasis in Matt. 5.45 is directly concerned with the stance of the enemy-lovers. Part of the scenario of enemy-love is concerned with responding in the situation to the God who makes the sun rise on the evil and the good, and sends rain on the just and on the unjust. In encountering opposition, one must be true to the Kingdom. In Matt. 5.44f. the community, in collision with its adversaries, must not even in such extremity deny its primary allegiance. It must radiate *shalom* (Matt. 5.9): blessing, not cursing. To prohibit the latter is to rule out both verbal abuse and social ostracism.[63] The community must reach out to those who oppose it, and always seek to 'overcome evil with good' (Rom. 12.21). Love to enemies is thus always in context with mission: the ultimate object is to win over those from whom one is alienated and so enable them to respond in trust to God and find salvation (cf. 1 Pet. 3.1).

At this point we appreciate that love to enemies, which makes such a demand of the lover, also places a demand on the enemy and on the situation of alienation that obtains between the two parties. What is now emerging is the description of a strategy by which the faith-community – powerless in so far as it has renounced all worldly power bases – can respond to the harassment, the discrimination, the active opposition of the various power groups, and in its response even work for good. The angle of strategy is particularly evident in the commentary on the *ius talionis* (or 'law of retribution')[64] given in Matt. 5.39–42. The passages from the Torah presuppose situations of violent dispute and the consequent necessity for punishment, retribution or recompense: i.e., the Scriptures are concerned for justice, law and order, and a criminal code. The concern of the New Testament community – prefigured in the disciples around Jesus and actualized in the church communities – was two-fold. One was concern within the community that an angry dispute should not lead to unforgiving attitudes or vengeance but should be resolved as quickly as possible within the community itself (cf. Matt. 5.22–6); the way to resolve it being not by legal casuistry[65] but through love and acceptance as the means of reconciliation. To seek legal redress is a defeat for the community (1 Cor. 6.7; cf. Matt. 5.40). 'Why not suffer wrong?', asks Paul. The apostolic plea stands in the tradition of Matt. 5.39: 'Do not resist one who is evil' – with the implication that the commended strategy brings victory for the community. The issue is not victory over the enemy (whom one is not to resist) but victory to the Kingdom of God (which may mean sacrifice on one's own part).

The second community concern, evident in Matthew, was the encounter with the violence offered to the community by outside agencies. In this case, non-resistance means the rejection of resistance by violence: the community renounces retaliation in kind when violence is offered: the strategy of the Kingdom is always to 'do good to those who hate you' (Luke 6.27; cf. Rom. 13.1; 1 Pet. 2.15). In the context of the disciple-community around Jesus, this is tantamount to the rejection of the Zealot option.[66] Of course, various non-violent alternatives enjoyed a measure of recognition in the ancient Jewish world, from general strike to corporate martyrdom.[67] But Jesus' teaching did not set out an ideology of passive resistance nor did it necessarily operate in terms of a principle of non-violence as such. Rather, it related to specific contexts, e.g., one in which violence is offered to the disciple, especially by a member of the military (cf. Matt. 5.41). The strategy of turning the other cheek (5.39) is a refusal to trade insults or blows, or to inflame the situation; it is to create a new situation by refusing to assent to the logic of violence. Non-resistance is here non-cooperation in violence. Similarly, going the second mile is to refuse to co-operate in the ploy by which the oppressor forces the role of victim on a subject people: one carries the burden freely and with dignity, and twice as far. Non-resistance to evil is itself a paradox. Matt. 5.39 cannot entail a total rejection of *every* type of resistance,[68] for this would fail to express the *counter*-force which the Kingdom of God constitutes.[69] Hence the examples in Matt. 5.39–42 embody a certain strain of resistance. Without this feature, non-resistance would be merely a gesture of political support for the *status quo*. The praxis of the Kingdom follows a different strategy. It is well exemplified by Martin Luther King's policy of non-cooperation with evil in the particularities of his situation.

That is not to make King's interpretation mandatory for all Christians today. Each context is distinct, and within it Christians have to discover the strategy that will most effectively combine love to enemies, non-cooperation with evil and the promotion of justice and right. This is no easy option, for – as is evident in the cross as well as in the teaching of Jesus – the price of the policy may have to be paid in personal suffering and risk. Hence discipleship is described in terms of taking up one's cross (cf. Matt. 8.34 par.). In this respect as in so many others, Jesus' enactment of the Kingdom in his own ministry was definitive.

(ii) THE ESTABLISHED AUTHORITIES AND THE COUNTER-FORCE OF THE KINGDOM. The death of John the Baptist at the hands of Herod amply illustrates how dangerous it was for a public figure to be openly critical of the political authorities, even in Galilee. It suggests that Jesus, whom Herod reportedly regarded as John *redivivus* (Mark 6.16; Matt. 14.2), would be constantly under surveillance. The case that Jesus was a political revolutionary, particularly with Zealot sympathies,[70] has not been substantiated, nor is it inherently likely.[71] But if Jesus was a liberationist whose ministry gave expression to the praxis of the Kingdom – and that is implicit in the argument of this book –

then his religious activity in itself expressed a *counter*-force directed at all oppressive forces, spiritual and material: as L. Schottroff has observed, 'Oppression by political masters and oppression by demons is on the same level and is dangerous and all-embracing'.[72] Since the Kingdom of God was also all-embracing, the potential for collision was enormous. Jesus' strategy appears to have been to concentrate on allowing the enactment of the Kingdom to open up new possibilities of understanding and action for those involved. The focus of the interaction was, as we have seen, the community around Jesus: the group whose awareness of the Kingdom was constantly challenged to expand and develop, even through experiences of alienation and disequilibrium. A partial similarity in group dynamic might be seen in the modern 'base communities' outlined by Ernesto Cardinal:[73] in both cases also, reflection and action are closely related. But this praxis inevitably led to the breaking of conventions and tabus, clashes with the guardians of the religious and sometimes the political *status quo*, frequent controversy and occasional social disturbance. Nevertheless, a certain *modus vivendi* seems to have been arrived at in Galilee. It was, as Matthew makes explicit (16.21), precisely when Jesus announced that he would press home his message on the Jerusalem establishment that the comprehension of the disciple-group was strained to the limit. Modern discussion frequently focuses on questions of Christology (son of man) and atonement in relation to the passion predictions.

What must not be overlooked is the awareness reflected in the Synoptic tradition of a collision between Jesus' ministry and the national (religious) structures of authority. Why *must* he go to Jerusalem? Evidently, because only there could he confront these structures. So the story proceeds with mounting tension until his arrival in the city. The story of the entry itself reflects conventional patterns and, in the form we have it, relates directly to the Evangelists' perspectives.[74] It is *possible* that the pattern reflected some kind of spontaneous enactment by Jesus' followers – a brief explosion of hope and fervour at an evocative point in their journey – and that such an enactment was related to the dynamics of the Kingdom, but the incident would be small in scale: the specific overtones of the Davidic Messiah are secondary. The cleansing of the temple, to which a high degree of probability attaches, is not (*pace* Brandon) a powerful physical assault by a strong force of freedom fighters, but a symbolic or parabolic enactment by Jesus. In expelling the traders, there is a brief enactment of scriptural fulfilment (cf. Zech. 14.21b), a performance of the new dynamic of the Kingdom (subsequently explored in terms of Isa. 56.7 and Jer. 7.11). The cursing of the fig-tree develops the parabolic performance of the Kingdom as the invasion of the new order and judgement on the old.[75] Its intimate connection with the cleansing of the temple underlies Jesus' challenge to the structures of the existing order. His performance of the Kingdom was bound to find flashpoints in the great symbols of the Jewish tradition: king, priest, temple, prophet, land... Each of these was highly charged; and Jesus' eschatological enactment tended to alienate not only the Jewish establishment but the anti-establishment as well. His message had as little comfort for the Zealots and the ascetics as it had for the Pharisees and Sadducees. His very presence expressed the challenge of the Kingdom: hence his determination to be present in Jerusalem and the concerted effort to be rid of him. Whether Jesus' execution was directly sanctioned by the Jews[76] or by the Romans (as the traditional story of the trial before Pilate suggests)[77] the *titulus* on the cross gives the last word, however ironically, to the counter-force: 'the King of the Jews' (cf. Mark 15.26; Matt. 27.37; Luke 23.38).

NOTES

1   Tracy (1978).
2   cf. Legasse (1969, 1970); Krause, ed. (1973).
3   cf. Black (1947).
4   Rawlinson (1925).
5   cf. Pedersen (1926); Jeremias (1960).
6   cf. Sauer (1981).
7   Robbins (1983).
8   op. cit., p. 53.
9   Silberman (1983), p. 115.
10 cf. Jeremias (1960); Lindars (1981).
11 It is often assumed that Mark 10.15/Luke 18.17 is a secondary and inferior version of Matt. 18.3. Lindars advanced four arguments. (a) The rhythm of Matthew's version is superior to Mark's. Even if this is true, it is not clear whether a firm conclusion can be drawn from it. (b) Mark's 'receive' is dictated by Mark 9.37 and makes the *logion*

'almost tautologous'. But it is by no means self-evident that Mark 9.37 is the source of Mark's expression here: the phrase has specific content in the Rabbinic tradition where 'to receive the Kingdom' is an accepted term meaning to recite the Shema and acknowledge the One God of Israel (cf. McDonald, 1973). (c) Lindars argues as follows: Mark 10.15 has the singular, 'like a *paidion*', although the context suggests the plural as more appropriate, hence 'the singular has been carried over from the source'. On the other hand, Matthew's version requires the plural 'like *paidia*'. If he were dependent on Mark, he would have retained Mark's indefinite 'whoever...' plus the singular '*paidion*'. One does not fault Lindars' conclusion that Matthew left his source intact. 'Like children' in 18.3 is the only such plural in the entire passage, and Matthew is able to incorporate it because, as we have seen, his method interposes the particular with the general, and the plural is acceptable as a generalized reference. But Lindars has already admitted that Mark's singular ('like a *paidion*') has been carried over from source. Hence the obvious conclusion is that Mark and Matthew are not dependent on each other at this point and, since neither produces the form which their contexts warrant, each must be dependent on a distinct source. The tradition has bifurcated before it reached them. (d) Finally, Lindars appeals strongly to the Semitism which is taken to underlie Matthew's 'turn and become', with the suggestion that it means 'become again'. If so, Mark 10.15 comes from a different realm of discourse: no less Semitic, close to the Rabbinic, and directly related to the problem of how one 'receives' the Kingdom of God. Attempts to take 18.3 as 'even more original' than Mark 10.15 (Crossan, 1983) invariably ignore this latter point. On the other hand, it is mere supposition that Matt. 18.3 is a Matthean attempt to clarify Mark 10.15, 'which may have seemed ambiguous or obscure' (Tannehill, 1983).

12   e.g. Clarke (1929); Schelling (1966).
13   op. cit. (1983).
14   op. cit. (1981).
15   Tannehill (1983).
16   cf. Weber (1979).
17   cf. Jung (2) (1968), pp. 151–81.
18   ibid., p. 161.
19   ibid., p. 162.
20   ibid., p. 164.
21   cf. A. Oepke, *TDNT* V. pp. 639–45.
22   Oepke, ibid., p. 649.
23   ibid.
24   cf. Via (1985), p. 130.
25   op. cit., p. 169.
26   op. cit., p. 13.
27   cf. Mussner (1959).
28   *contra* Best (1981).
29   cf. Kee (1963).

30   cf. Flender (1967).
31   cf. Conzelmann (1960).
32   Tugwell (1980), p. 16.
33   Jeremias (1969), pp. 122f.; Mealand (1980).
34   cf. 1QHod. 2.34f.; 4Qp Ps.37; 1QS 4.2–6.
35   cf. Dupont (1973), pp. 385–471.
36   cf. Stendahl (1962); Burchard (1978), p. 57.
37   One might point to the following evidence. The criterion of multiple
     attestation is abundantly met. The criterion of differentiation is
     partially satisfied by the fact that Christian paraenesis preferred to
     emphasize love to neighbour by itself (cf. Gal. 5.14; Rom. 13.9; Jas. 2.8;
     cf. Matt. 19.19). The problem lies in the area of Judaism (Fuller [1978],
     p. 47), where instances of the twin commandment in Test. Issachar
     (5.2, 7.6) and Test. Dan (5.3) suggest an affinity between the gospel
     source and Palestinian or even Hellenistic Judaism (the boundary
     between the two being now much less clear than was once thought to
     be the case). Even if the evidence of the Aramaic Testament of Levi
     from Cave 4 at Qumran tilts the balance in favour of a Palestinian
     origin, there remains the question of whether it can be ascribed to
     Jesus in particular. At this point, R. H. Fuller introduces the criterion
     of coherence, but strangely refuses to develop the notion of the
     coherence of the primary commandment with the admittedly central
     notion of 'the inbreaking of the Kingdom of God' on the curious
     grounds that the post-Easter community was 'concerned to associate
     the love commandment with the eschatological proclamation' (p. 51).
     In other words, Christian preaching (it is suggested) related the love
     commandment to the 'eschatological event' of Christ, but Jesus did
     not relate it to the Kingdom of God – in spite of Mark 12.28–34 and
     the tenor of his parabolic teaching. Instead, Fuller prefers to underline
     the affinity of Jesus' teaching with the wisdom tradition, as in the
     Testaments of the Twelve Patriarchs. Yet the present enactment of the
     Kingdom by Jesus is demonstrably the most characteristic feature of
     his teaching, and the Marcan tradition underlines the coherence of the
     twin commandment with the dynamics of the Kingdom. Both in
     the enactment of the Kingdom and in the moral response to it, the
     common factor is the sovereign will of God (cf. Mark 12.32). To ascribe
     the citing of the Shema (Mark 12.29) to the secondary need to enlighten
     Gentile readers (so Bornkamm, 1957; Furnish, 1973; Fuller) is to miss
     the valid insight it affords into Jesus' hermeneutical procedures. The
     Marcan insight is that Jesus accepts that there are hermeneutical
     priorities (cf. Mark's 'first' and 'second' commandment) in the
     interpretation of the law, and Deut. 6.4f. is identified as a focus of such
     priority. This hermeneutical exactitude is more evident in Jesus than
     in the Testaments and very much more evident than in Hellenistic
     Jewish writers such as Aristeas or Philo (cf. Becker, 1970; Slingerland,
     1977; Fuller, p. 48f.). Nor does the relative down-grading of cultic
     observance in Mark argue for a Hellenistic provenance: the acme of
     this tradition is the well-attested cleansing of the temple in Jesus'

ministry. Indeed, to assign Mark's pericope to a Hellenistic provenance is to rob it of much of its significance (see concluding chapter, below). In short, to adopt Fuller's solution is to resort to a scarcely conceivable separation of ethics and eschatology in the teaching of Jesus.

38 Driver, *Deuteronomy* (ICC), ad loc.
39 Gerhardssohn (1982), p. 47.
40 So Furnish (1973), following Bornkamm.
41 op. cit., p. 28f.
42 cf. Minear (1972).
43 cf. Furnish, op. cit.
44 cf. Fairweather and McDonald (1984), pp. 82–5.
45 *Gospel and Law* (1951), p. 42.
46 cf. Fletcher (1966).
47 Via (1985), pp. 85f.
48 ibid., p. 86.
49 cf. Lehmann (1976), p. 124.
50 cf. Hengel (1981).
51 cf. Tannehill (1980).
52 'They left their nets and followed him' (Mark 1.18; Matt. 4.20); 'they left the boat and their father and followed him' (Matt. 4.22; cf. Mark 1.20); 'he left everything, and rose and followed him' (Luke 5.28; cf. Mark 2.14; Matt. 9.9).
53 cf. Mackey (1979); Jeremias (1967).
54 cf. Kelber (1983), pp. 96f.
55 Perrin (1967), p. 102.
56 ibid., p. 103.
57 cf. Kelber, op. cit., p. 126.
58 cf. Crossan (1975).
59 Mackey (1979), p. 150.
60 cf. Hooker (1983), p. 49.
61 cf. Piper (1979), pp. 49–65.
62 Schottroff (1978), p. 12.
63 ibid., p. 23.
64 cf. Exod. 21.24; Lev. 24.20; Deut. 19.21.
65 cf. Braun (1969), p. 125.
66 cf. Hengel (1971), p. 28; Lührmann, *ZTK* 69 (1972), p. 437.
67 cf. Yoder (1972), pp. 90–3.
68 cf. Schottroff, op. cit., p. 27.
69 cf. Schottroff (1984), p. 71.
70 cf. Bammel (1984), pp. 11–68.
71 *contra* Brandon (1967); cf. Sweet (1984), pp. 1–9.
72 Schottroff, op. cit., p. 69.
73 1977–82.
74 Catchpole (1984).
75 Telford (1980); Bammel (1984), pp. 124ff.
76 Bammel, op. cit., p. 445.
77 cf. Luke 23.2ff., Schneider (1984).

5

Conclusion

1 THE NOTION OF PERFORMANCE: USEFULNESS AND LIMITATIONS

A bivalent understanding of performance has been developed in this volume, in order to describe Jesus' preaching of the Kingdom both as a set of motifs which he framed into coherent discourse, and as a thematic address which he designed to revise his hearers' ethics. Although literary theory proved useful in the development of our approach, 'performance' here has been a heuristic category, discovered less by theory than by our reading of the Synoptics, which was refined to take account of features of the texts which have been considered. In just this sense, our procedure has been exegetical, rather than synthetic. But 'performance', whether at the level of motif or of theme, is susceptible of wider meanings. The purpose of this chapter is to consider how some of those meanings might be taken further in analysing Jesus' construal of the Kingdom, and where caution must be exercised in order to avoid the unwarranted imputation of a modern idea to ancient texts. As is by now a habit (cf. Chapters one and two), the performance of motifs will be dealt with first, and then the performance of themes.

2 THE PERFORMANCE OF MOTIFS

Narrative metaphor proved the best designation for those parables of Jesus which are not simply figurative sayings, but develop their address to the hearer by means of story and image. Within the corpus of early Judaism (Jesus' sayings included), that genre of discourse appears quite plain, as distinct from proverb, aphorism, instruction, debate, and announcement. The precise delineation of these genres lies outside our present purpose; the striking feature from our point of view is that the telling and retelling of a parable involves a degree of deliberative choice. Speaker and hearer must adjust the way they talk and listen, if communication is to occur.

The most obvious adjustment involved is the acceptance of metaphor as a means of conveying what is spoken. Referential notions of language must be relaxed, so that the metaphorical figure might be developed and appreciated. The question of how the metaphor relates to what can be perceived is held in abeyance, until the image is fully developed. The development of that image, in turn, relies on narrative means, and the unfolding of plot requires a further suspension of the referential function of language. Reference to the received understanding of reality will not be evident word by word, but only after the narrative metaphor has become whole. The tension between image and reference will appear all the more extreme when the speaker stresses the realism of his discourse: the more realistic an image appears, the more pressing the issue of its relevance becomes. That tension is a striking feature of Jesus' parables.

The description of performance as a selection of linguistic choices in speaking is reminiscent of Linnemann's assessment of the parables under the category of 'language event'.[1] Both 'performance' and 'language event' refer to the use of motifs to offer a fresh account of something which referential speech cannot, or does not, convey. As we saw in Chapter two, however, Linnemann's construction is of an existentialist nature. Language is conceived of as what gives life possibility, so that a parable compels a decision for or against the possibility conveyed. Linnemann is indebted to Jeremias for her emphasis on decision, and it is quite unclear what she (or he) would make of that emphasis in respect of early Jewish parables. Outside the presupposition of a basic assent to Christology, in other words, 'language event' ceases to function as a category of analysis. The notion of 'performance' does not require an existentialist or christological presupposition in order to be applied. It stands or falls only according to its adequacy as an account of the linguistic choices implicit in speech.[2]

John Dominic Crossan, whose description of metaphor has

already proved useful in this study, has also turned his attention to the question of performance. He does so in a volume dedicated to the aphorisms of Jesus, but the phenomenon he describes is surely applicable to the corpus of Jesus' sayings generally. In his formulation,[3] the oral transmission of a saying is designed to convey its sense, and must be distinguished from the scribal attempt to record actual words. Much as in the work of Werner Kelber, albeit less programmatically, Crossan investigates the particular question of the transmission of sayings as represented within the Gospels, where oral and scribal mentalities both seem to be in effect. The line of demarcation between the two, of course, is difficult to draw, even in the most general of terms: there is a point at which variation in wording in any medium of transmission will alter the sense an originating speaker attempted to convey. Moreover, Rabbinic tradents placed great store by verbal accuracy in oral transmission. Variations within Rabbinica in the presentation of the same basic saying demonstrate that sense was not the slave of diction alone among the rabbis,[4] but verbatim agreement among differing presentations is also a commonly found feature.[5] Indeed, the very fact that the Rabbinic corpus is a literature suggests that oral and written transmission were complementary procedures. It is reasonable to distinguish between them, as Crossan does, but it is also necessary to bear in mind both that a *writer* within early Judaism might be truer to sense than to wording, and that an *oral tradent* might seek – and achieve – verbatim repetition.

Crossan uses the word 'performance' to describe the differing ways an oral tradent might formulate a saying. More precisely, he describes such performances as 'performancial variations'.[6] The variations might involve such phenomena as abbreviation, expansion, grammatical conversion, synonymous expression, and transposition, all of which have been commonly observed by form critics, folklorists, and students of Rabbinica. The important point for Crossan is that performative changes of this kind are to be distinguished from 'hermeneutical variations', which involve a change of meaning.[7]

In Chapter one, we observed that Crossan considers the aggressive formulation of the golden rule to be a 'performancial variation' of the aphorism, 'What you hate, do not do to any-

one.'[8] To his mind, this is an instance of conversion, from a
negative to a positive formulation.[9] Such an analysis misses the
obvious point that the positive wording of Jesus' teaching carries
a nuance which is absent in undeniably similar statements:
one's love becomes an incitement to action, where elsewhere
one's taste serves as a restraint on behaviour. What is a nuance
at the level of motif is more significant at the level of theme: the
ethical demand positively to seek the good one wishes on behalf
of others is clearly more dynamic than a call for restraint. That
would appear to be more than a matter of 'performancial
variation'; the substance of what is conveyed is distinctive.[10]

There are instances in which the move from a positive to a
negative formulation does not affect meaning. In Matt. 7.17–18,
the statement about good and rotten trees is simply reinforced
by the conversion (cf. Luke 6:43). Crossan is therefore correct
in so far as the shift concerned might represent a 'performancial
variation', but the golden rule is not a good instance of the
phenomenon. The case illustrates what Crossan recognizes
generally,[11] that performancial and hermeneutical variations are
not always to be distinguished easily, by means of formal
considerations alone.

Crossan's volume is of signal value, in demonstrating that
the oral and scribal transmission which produced the Gospels
generated varied, but coherent, accounts of Jesus' teaching.
Within the sayings which concern him, he distinguishes
'aphoristic core' from the performancial and hermeneutical
variations of the core.[12] In the case of his treatment of the golden
rule, however, we have seen that Jesus' actual statement is
treated, not as a 'core', but as a performancial variant of an early
Jewish maxim. It would seem that Crossan conceives of
'aphoristic core', not as an actual instance of speech, but as the
underlying structure which a speaker exploits.[13]

Performance is more usefully conceived of as the articulation
of motifs in order to convey meaning: it is a speaker's enactment
of possibilities that concerns us, not, in the first instance, a
theoretical description of what those possibilities might have
been.[14] Language only constitutes an aesthetic object which
can be perceived when it is performed on a specific occasion.
Hearers can only hear when something is said, not when
possibilities remain pre-conscious. Once speech occurs, of course,

hearers respond to it on the basis of their own linguistic experience, but speech alone occasions that process. Accordingly, a performance is not a set of variants on a 'core', but an irreducible unit of communication. What is said is the proper concern of exegesis, not what might alternatively have been said. In the case of Jesus' sayings, the only 'core' is the performance of motifs, not a catalogue of possibilities.

The genre of a saying, whether parabolic, aphoristic, proverbial, paraenetic, controversial, or declarative, constitutes a major criterion of the performance achieved. Generic selection exploits conventions of speech accessible to speaker and hearer alike, but genres do not exist in the abstract, any more than motifs do. Speaker, motif, and genre interact in a process as mysterious as that depicted in the parable of the man, the seed, and the earth. As in the case of that parable, we understand *what* happens, but not *how* it happens. The wording of the same performance might vary – and, given the exigencies of human communication, must do so – but variation of that sort is incidental to the meaning conveyed. The performed meaning, for that reason, is an appropriate object of exegetical inquiry.

3 THE PERFORMANCE OF THEMES

The initial question posed in this volume concerned the nexus, if any, between 'eschatology' and 'ethics' in Jesus' teaching. Those two categories represent distinctions made among sayings on the basis of their content. Content is an obvious criterion for distinguishing sayings, but there has been a tendency to bifurcate Jesus' position by erecting his 'eschatology' on the foundation of some material, and his 'ethics' on the foundation of other material. Our analysis of certain parables, however, has suggested that eschatological motifs are cognate with ethical themes. Moreover, we have suggested that explicitly moral instructions, most notably the commandment to love in its various forms, arise out of an underlying understanding that God is eschatologically active. Formally, that is just our solution to the problem, or the apparent problem, which modern scholarship has posed. Eschatological motifs and ethical themes are aspects of a single vision of God's ultimate action in the world.

The interface between motif and theme is evidenced within the early Jewish genre of parable generally, and cannot be claimed as Jesus' invention. His creativity, the *ipsissima vox Jesu*, lies more in the manner of articulating motifs and implying themes than in the act of co-ordinating them. In the first half of the nineteenth century, Jakob Friedrich Fries argued on a philosophical basis that ethics regularly derives from a motival – or, as he said, aesthetic – perception: one's intimation of the 'sublime' becomes the basis on which one acts. The question obviously emerges, What is the sublime, on which good action is predicated, and by whose standard some behaviour is proscribed? To Fries' mind, the very form of that question proves that aesthetics, the issue of what is perceived, is prior to the question of ethics, which concerns the enactment which follows that perception.[15]

During the course of the century, Kant – of course – proved far more influential than Fries, and deeply marked the development of theology. By the time Albrecht Ritschl came to formulate a definition of the Kingdom in Jesus' preaching, the result was classically Kantian: the Kingdom referred at one and the same time to the good willed by God to people, and their common task of enacting that good.[16] Ritschl's definition in fact allowed of a transcendent aspect, in the divine will to good, but its immanent emphasis, on the human task of doing good, is evident. Moreover, because the very notion of moral good is only formally transcendent, but practically apprehensible and realizable within the world of people, its divine source is easily overlooked. When, on the basis of his study of early Jewish eschatology, Johannes Weiss insisted that the transcendent must be seen as having pre-eminence in Jesus' preaching of the Kingdom, he did so in conscious opposition to Ritschl.[17]

Given the Kantian terms of reference within which Ritschl and Weiss operated, disagreement was inevitable. Ritschl emphasized the moral and immanent, Weiss the aesthetic and transcendent, aspects of the Kingdom. What was for Ritschl ethical and practical was for Weiss eschatological and esoteric. Their underlying agreement lay in the assumption that human reason did not function in both ways at once. The vigour of their assumption proved even more influential among their successors. From Ritschl's approach, the movement of a 'social gospel' emerged: with great urgency, teachers such as Shailer Mathews and Walter Rauschenbusch insisted that the preaching of the Kingdom implied a programme for the modern world.[18] Under the sway of Weiss, the school of 'consistent eschatology' developed: Albert Schweitzer and Rudolf Bultmann so insisted on Jesus' orientation towards God's ultimate, and near, future, that an immediate interest in ethics on his part was precluded.

The obvious antagonism between these two perspectives is to some extent belied by the *rapprochement* approximated by some of the best of their representatives. Trained at the University of Chicago (where Mathews had earlier taught), Charles Chester McCown was highly effective in the attempt to construe Jesus' preaching with reference to the social world of his time. McCown, an excellent scholar of both the New Testament and Judaism, recognized the centrality of eschatological language during the time of Jesus, and in his preaching. Within McCown's approach, however, the function of eschatology in Jesus' message was to underline the urgently moral challenge he posed.[19] Although such attempts, as described in Chapter one, fail to give Jesus' promulgation of the Kingdom the foundational importance it exegetically requires, McCown nonetheless signalled a willingness to reconcile ethics and eschatology, albeit by means of subsuming the latter within the former. In Germany, Rudolf Otto contributed a seminal study of both the Kingdom of God and the phrase, 'the son of man'. Otto was heavily influenced by the *religionsgeschichtliche* movement, and argued that such language was to be derived from Zoroastrian eschatology. Owing to the difficulty of establishing a firm connection between the New Testament and the Zoroastrian corpus, and even of dating these Persian documents, Otto's argument has not won wide acceptance.[20] But the insight Otto gained from these sources, whatever their date, was that the eschatological expectations of Zoroastrians were not merely theoretical. The ultimate victory of Ahura Mazda, the divine redeemer, over Ormudz, his satanic antagonist, was to be shared by followers of Zoroaster by means of their commitment to moral light, rather than darkness. The notion that ancient texts might develop their sense in the bivalent performance of expectation and ethics, motif and theme, opened an eschatological construal of Jesus' message to the sort of moral understanding which Schweitzer opposed.

An underlying influence of importance in Otto's career was the thought of Fries, which we mentioned at the beginning of this section. Among Otto's earlier works, perhaps the most significant was an analysis of religious philosophy on a Friesian basis (1931). He focused on what he called 'the idea of the holy', or 'the numinous', as the ground of religious perception, and of action undertaken on that basis. What for Fries was an intimation of the sublime, became for Otto a quasi-substantial phenomenon, the holy as an object of experience. Given Otto's phenomenological bent, his increasing emphasis on what was perceived, rather than on the qualities and ethical results of experience, appears quite natural. But as compared to others, such as Bultmann, who pursued an eschatological understanding of Jesus' teaching, he continued to urge a greater emphasis on the moral consequences of the Kingdom. Above all, he achieved a focus on the Kingdom, rather than Christology, as the centre of Jesus' thought: 'Jesus did not "bring" the kingdom, and that idea was foreign to him; it was rather the kingdom which brought Jesus with itself.' That sentence, which was cited and approved of by Dodd,[21] expressed the most important insight about the Kingdom which discussion between the wars achieved. Had it been understood as frequently as it was quoted, the attempt to decipher eschatology in terms of Christology would sooner have been recognized as the exegetical failure which it is.

Exegetically, of course, it is impossible to demonstrate that the Kingdom was an eschatological idea of the holy which pressed those who perceived it to ethical action. Whether 'the holy' is a phenomenon of human experience, susceptible of description, remains an open question. By the same token, Fries' claim that ethical action is a function of aesthetic cognition is no more than a possibility. The Kantian distinction between 'pure', or cognitive, reason, and 'practical', or moral, reason continues to attract support, although those who accept it are obliged, as Fries felt, to explain the relationship between the two within a single human subject. The notion of 'performance' does not demand a specific philosophical framework, any more than it requires a particular linguistic framework. The notion might be employed to investigate philosophical possibilities, but its initial function is to describe the relationship between eschatology and ethics in early Judaism and the preaching of Jesus.

A limitation of restraint, then, is appropriate philosophically, just as it is linguistically. In neither case should 'performance' be taken to presume a specific system of analysis or understanding. The fact remains, however, that a bivalent construal of performance does allow of the development of ethical themes by means of eschatological motifs. The emphasis throughout is on the divine, eschatological action on which ethical response is predicated, so that the fundamental character of performance is transcendent. Jesus' preaching of the Kingdom is in the first place an announcement of God's dynamic rule. Human response, which might generally be described under the category of repentance, is performed as response, not as initiating cause. The fact that, humanly speaking, the Kingdom is normally a challenge of the future, removes the possibility of understanding it within immanental terms of reference alone. The Kingdom is immanent only in so far as God's rule impinges upon, and elicits a response from, those who live in the present. At the same time, the Kingdom cannot be reduced to human expectations of the future, any more than it can be reduced to human activities in the present: the temporal ambivalence of the Kingdom in Jesus' preaching is redolent of its transcendent character. Its future and present aspects require theologically to be retained, lest the Kingdom be equated with purely human, apocalyptic schemes, or with purely human, social programmes.

The inadequacy of the movement for a 'social gospel' has become an axiom of theology in the twentieth century. Those influenced by Karl Barth strenuously argued that it failed to do justice to the otherness of God, and its optimism made little sense of a world which turned more readily to war than to the challenge of God's Kingdom. But its recognized failure has brought a reluctance to perceive the dimension of response to the Kingdom which Jesus insisted upon. In that sense, Schweitzer's scheme caught the tenor of our time, but fails in its exegesis of texts. The Kingdom of God is indeed transcendent, but it is not irrelevant. The ethical themes of Jesus' parables do not reduce the Kingdom to an immanental programme of reform, but they do convey the Kingdom as a transcendental impingement on human behaviour in the world of immanence. To put the matter more simply: as the Kingdom refers to divine action, it calls for cognate, human action, without betraying its divine source.

The human action concerned is presented by Jesus as an assent to the Kingdom as supremely valuable, which implies a penitential devaluation of everything else. Readiness to respond to the Kingdom, to be caught up in the world of parable, involves a willingness to relax one's hold on those enjoyments and commitments which are a part of received reality. More positively, the agreement to act upon the Kingdom, to perform analogously to what is conveyed in parable, constitutes an assent to the Kingdom as a reality within and behind actuality as one normally perceives it. Any good idea can be enjoyed: when acted upon, the message of the Kingdom is implicitly accepted as both good and effectual. At this point, it becomes clear that the ethical performance of the Kingdom is no denial of its transcendence. On the contrary, because the Kingdom strikes the hearer as discognate with received reality, and yet inceptively present, action is the sole means of assenting to it. Inaction would signal an acceptance only of what is commonly regarded as real; ethical performance is the sign that parabolic performance has succeeded, because the hearer enacts the transcendent activity he perceives. Precisely because the Kingdom is not an entity, but dynamic transcendence, its ethical enactment and its perception occur in a single movement.

What makes the transcendence of the Kingdom dynamic is its susceptibility to performance immanentally, within the terms of received reality. But the notion of ethical performance is no more immanental than that of cognitive performance: at both levels, the single point remains that the transcendent, divine rule impinges on what we see. However active the human performance of the Kingdom might be, it appears as parabolic enactment of a prior, divine performance. Any retreat from performance, as perception and enactment, would not make the Kingdom appear *more* transcendent. The reverse is rather the case: the alternative to a performative model is a theoretical one, in which the Kingdom is equated with human expectation. Precisely that strategy was proposed by Schweitzer and Bultmann. The result was not a theological evaluation of the Kingdom, but a denial that it had any meaning in modern terms, since eschatology was utterly conditioned by historical factors which no longer obtain. There is nothing more immanental and transient than human hopes and dreams, however much wishful thinking gives them the aura of transcendence.

The Kingdom of God is an inceptive and ultimate disclosure of the divine, whose orientation is irreducibly towards the future. But, as disclosed transcendence, the Kingdom is also immanent, the impingement of a new rule on what we normally accept. Because that is the case, assent to the Kingdom can never be merely propositional. To assent to the idea, say, of transcendence revealed in immanence, without enacting the new reality affected, is to cherish a dream, not to perceive a fresh reality. Whoever perceives God ultimately revealing himself in the world must – if he is sincere – behave in that world, for good and all, as a new person. He *is* a new person, whose citizenship has been changed irrevocably.

4 PERFORMANCE AS SIGN

'No sign will be given to this generation...' (Mark 8.12 par.). The performance of the Kingdom is neither contrived nor theatrical. It is not merely a 'wonder', although it can be described in that way when its newness or unexpectedness evokes astonishment or reveals unforeseen dimensions. In Kingdom discourse, an authentic sign is a performative action which has a transcendental reference. Such actions have four primary characteristics. (i) They are performed in response to the dynamic and transcendent Kingdom of God: hence the importance of the baptism story for the ministry of Jesus, with its motif of commissioning by God through his Spirit (Mark 1.9ff., par.). (ii) They are performed in response to human need and as an expression of the 'wholeness' (*shalom*) of God's creation. (iii) They are performed in demonstration of the dynamic Kingdom – 'in demonstration of the Spirit and of power' (Paul: 1 Cor. 2.4) – whence are derived motifs of the Kingdom.

(iv) They are performed as an invitation or summons to respond in repentance and faith, to 'become as a child' and grow as a child of God. In what context, then, should the reader appropriate these characteristics?

Significant action of this kind presupposes effective communication. It is not a matter of the mere communication of data: the 'banking' type of knowledge transmission,[22] which has dominated Western learning from Greco-Roman times. If it were so, then the Kingdom would be reduced to a form of *gnosis*, a body of knowledge prized for its efficacy. Interpretations which systematically analyse 'the message of the parables of Jesus' in terms of propositional statements of a theological or christological kind, as Jeremias tends to do,[23] are in danger of being entrapped in this model. The type of communication presupposed by Kingdom language involves reception, participation and reorientation on the part of the receptor in relation to the reality that is being communicated. It thus involves existential encounter in the tradition of Kierkegaard and Buber. It is a demanding type of communication, for it entails encounter with a reality that transcends what we actually are and compels change in us even as it comes to us and even if we reject it: we are never quite the same persons after such an encounter. This is one way of expressing the *transcendent* and *dynamic* nature of the Kingdom. It also indicates the fact that to encounter the Kingdom is an event, a happening, which transforms our lives and points us towards a new way of life. 'Newness of life' is itself a sign of the Kingdom: 'the works of God' are manifest in us. Hence, the performance of the Kingdom embraces both divine initiative and human response, both motif making and thematic expression.

Such a comprehensive notion of the communication of the Kingdom must not ignore the fact that modern people encounter the tradition of the Kingdom in written form, two thousand years after the original event. What was of immediate concern to the ancient hearers may seem so distant from modern readers that it represents an alien world from which they are essentially excluded.[24] What then happens to the dynamic operation of the Kingdom? Gospel material was, of course, reshaped or re-presented, as the original context of the ministry of Jesus was superseded by the new and different contexts of the ministry of the early churches. Too often, scholars have taken this as a challenge merely to strip away the 'secondary' presentation (sometimes indicated by allegorizing of the parable) in order to recover the *Sitz im Leben Jesu*.[25] But the reason for the recasting of the parable in the early Church was precisely to *preserve* its performative character. The re-presentation recognized the immediacy of the message of the Kingdom for the new hearers. It combined freedom to adapt the parabolic materials with respect for the essential motifs and above all for the parabolic dynamics, and it became counter-productive only when those features were lost. Transmission therefore paradoxically involves respect for the givenness of the material and liberty to re-present it in order to attain the dynamic interaction with the audience, which is the point of the operation.

The writing of the Gospels exerted an element of control over the transmission of the tradition. For centuries, however, the Gospels were read aloud in church (Lat., *recitare*) and thus 'heard' rather than 'read' in the modern sense. The potential hazards of the written source – rigidity and 'data bank' views of knowledge – could therefore be obviated in the oral presentation, so that the dynamic element of transcendental encounter through the material at least to some extent remained a possibility. This is or can be true of 'the ministry of the Word' in liturgical practice today. Far reaching developments in the faith of the Church, however, tended to divert attention from the language of Kingdom to other forms of discourse,[26] while the Latin Church of the West in particular lost the immediacy of encounter for which the spoken language of the audience is an essential tool. Although this element was recovered in Reformation times, it was in the context of the rise of literacy in the wake of the Renaissance and the dissemination of printed books. A new era had dawned: the age of the reader had arrived;[27] and the reader was inducted with much expedition into the dogmatic systems of the Reformed Churches in particular. Generally speaking the language of the Kingdom was made to operate in dogmatic, christological and ethical contexts, without recovering the dynamics of parabolic discourse, as in the Gospels.

It is paradoxical that it is only as the age of literacy entered the period of its eclipse that scholarly attention has begun to be devoted to the understanding of the process of reading reception.[28] In place of the notion of the book as a coded repository of information provided by the author, requiring that the reader follow out the author's intention or substantiate the sources of the material, there has been a recovery of interest both in the operation of the text itself (e.g., as narrative) in relation to the reader and in the active part the reader plays in the process. In other words, the focus is now on communication and on the dynamic interaction of the reader and the world of the text or 'the intratextual narrative world'. There is no opportunity here to discuss in detail the problems and possibilities of the application of reading reception theory to the New Testament.[29] Clearly, the emergence of this interactive view of the reader's role has a cultural affinity with the development of the inter-active, performative view of parabolic operations outlined in this book: a shared debt to existentialism may be a significant link. What is of moment is that reception theory and our per-formative view of parables and Kingdom material combine to place emphasis upon response as an essential part of the experience or event.

Response, like performance and event itself, always occurs in a particular situation or context. The intratextual narrative world intimates something of the performative settings in the ministry of Jesus and reflects some early church contexts. Modern readers are brought into a similar kind of dialogue in their contemporary situations and confront the issues that are opened up for them. Here then is a new event, a modern event, in which the motifs of the Kingdom engage people in a radically different situation from the original performance, and evoke new responses. There are some common factors among these responses: the motifs consistently evoke repentance, not 'hard-heartedness'; love, rather than hate, bitterness or indifference; faith, trust and hope, rather than suspicion or despair; com-munity, rather than self-seeking or individualism; self-giving, rather than material advantage; and so on. But these positive responses never become principles in themselves, for to regard them as such would be to reduce or eliminate the central dynamic of the Kingdom which evokes them. It is also import-ant not to stop short at the level of generalization, as much twentieth-century dialectical theology tended to do. 'Performance' entails response-action which is grounded in historical existence. Hence, the responsive performance given to the Kingdom today must relate directly to the context of modern life. It has little to do with sentimental pilgrimages to the Holy Land, or archaeological reconstructions of life in Palestine two thousand years ago. It has everything to do with 'doing the will of God' today – and doing it to the glory of God, for the good of our neighbour, and as a 'sign' to the 'wicked and adulterous' world of today.

A little publication entitled *The Kingdom of God in North East England Today*[30] provides interesting illustration of our thesis. Approximately a dozen examples are cited of how various groups and people have responded to the dynamic of the Kingdom in their own modern situations. The examples themselves range from projects to sell third-world goods and to promote thoughtful buying (rather than 'shop around' consumerism) to far-reaching projects to create work for the unemployed; from campaigning to preserve a rural school, with its distinctive ethos and values, to the creation of a retreat house for spiritual renewal. The reader can hardly escape the conclusion that, while the traditional motifs of the Kingdom in the gospel parables remain constant, the response to them in modern situations can be as varied and creatively imaginative as the original performance was in Jesus' ministry. Hence modern issues arising out of engagement with the Kingdom will create new motifs, as signs to the modern age. For example, the image of the workshop where skills are acquired – whether the provision is by the state or Church or other organization — may be more pregnant with meaning today than that of the messianic banquet. It is not only a sign that someone cares or that people have value; it is an effective sign of acceptance, hope and purpose in life: i.e., a sign which actually effects what it points to. It witnesses to the possibility of transcending the prison-house of one's present existence and begins to realize it; and it does so as part of the dynamic of the Kingdom that is itself transcendent and imparts the power to transcend.

5 PERFORMANCE AND HUMAN DEVELOPMENT

Performance is a dynamic, interactive reality. It stands in tension with static, general concepts such as 'man' and 'modern man' which have figured largely in theological debate. Performance has to do with persons in action and interaction. A person is one who is constantly growing and developing and whose personal growth and development are stimulated by interaction with others, in community.[31] Our contention here, therefore, is that since performance is bound up with personhood, and since persons are by nature developmental, the level of performance at any given point should be susceptible of analysis in developmental terms. This is not to introduce an alien element into the debate, nor to subject Kingdom material to external constraint. It is to pursue the dialogue of theory and praxis in a real life context and so counteract and obviate the tendency to static thinking. As we shall see, the language and operation of the Kingdom not only reinforce the interactive notion of personhood but also demonstrate that the dynamics of transcendence are of critical importance in human development.

In the context of general developmental theory, James W. Fowler investigated the structures of faith development and produced a sixfold stage pattern which underlies and informs our present discussion. Fowler uses 'faith' to denote 'our way of finding coherence in and giving expression to the multiple forces and relations that make up our lives'.[32] Since Jesus' first proclamation of the Kingdom occurs in Mark in the context of 'believing in the gospel' (Mark 1.15), there is clearly a close correlation between the Kingdom and faith.

As far as young children are concerned (we may call this stage 1 or earlier), the Kingdom is God's gift, coming as blessing. Blessing implies the future as gift (cf. Gen. 12.1–3). It also implies that their present existence, with its freedom from adult cares and its natural responsiveness, is an expression of human flourishing ('theirs is the Kingdom'!) which adults, more mature in many ways, must recapture if they too are to enjoy the blessings of the Kingdom.

It is characteristic of older children (stage 2) to live their story: not to distance themselves from it by reflecting on it, but to be totally involved in it. Jesus encountered many people in the particularities of their own 'story' and at the point of their specific need: those suffering from leprosy and other diseases, the possessed and distracted, the fearful and inadequate. To them the Kingdom came as God's power of healing and restoration, the power of *shalom* that opens up the future in a new way. It may be observed that, under pressure of illness and anxiety, people tend to regress to a stage 2 position, becoming absorbed in what is happening to them: i.e., in their own story. But as with young children, some characteristics of this stage illustrate the pattern of discipleship: like the single-minded devotion of the servant boy Jesus set in the midst. Adults are not challenged to regress to this stage (as they may do in their weakness) but to recapture its most positive features ('Unless you become like this serving boy...').

Characteristically, adolescents, like many adults, put great store by inter-personal relationships and the conventional *mores* of their group (stage 3). Jesus, indeed, endorsed the importance of *koinonia*, the act of being together in fellowship, although it tended to become a deeper issue with him; yet there is no mistaking his enthusiasm for celebration – 'a winebibber', said his enemies. Many parables draw their theme from this inter-personal area and develop the appropriate issue from it. Critical appraisal of merely conformist stances, however, and new insights into the Kingdom take us into the stage 4 realm of discourse, characterized by Fowler as 'individuative reflective'. Indeed, when table fellowship becomes an issue – e.g., Who should sit at table? Who should be excluded? What has this to do with the Kingdom? – we may begin to see 'natural' human development under challenge from the transcendent. There are, of course, dangers. The critic can be arrogant: 'puffed up', in Pauline terminology. It is only through engagement with the transcendent that one can hope to come to terms with the further insights of stage 5, when one can begin to face up to the paradoxes of human existence while remaining true to one's highest perceptions of truth. Thus Jesus, confronted with the issue of the undeserved suffering of those on whom the tower of Siloam fell, rejects any form of slick theodicy, and accepts the paradox of seemingly unjust events in life in relation to the divine rule, but insists that one must respond, as ever, to the Kingdom in repentance and faith.

There is, therefore, an affinity between the 'natural' or created order and the working of the Kingdom: that is why Jesus can find so many parabolic themes in the created order. Nevertheless, 'natural' development – environmentally grounded – only takes us a limited way in personal maturation. The challenge of the transcendent is essential to further development – 'further' being determined by the point to which 'natural' development has brought one (most often, stage 2 or stage 3). While it is undoubtedly true that the challenge of the transcendent can take many forms,[33] the kind of operation which the parables of Jesus represent is integral to faith development. To be sure, the earlier stages produce their own parabolic images – becoming as a *paidion*, whether in the sense of a child (stage 1) or a servant (stage 2). But these images are so powerful because they pose the challenge of the transcendent not to young children but to adults, entrenched in their resistant egotism or in failure and defeatism. They present the challenge and opportunity both to 'de-centre' and to 're-centre' one's life – to lay it down so that one can find it again. Each stage has its in-built defence mechanism, its resistance to challenge or correction. Children can be quarrelsome and imperious, dissolving their games in disagreements (cf. Matt. 11.16–19; Luke 7.31–35). People can build completely false goals into their life-story, and live and die in pursuit of them: wealth, prestige, status, power, and so on. These must be abandoned and life re-centred if the Kingdom is to be entered. Table fellowship, which can express community at a potentially deep level, can also be made the prerogative of an exclusive group, closed to the rest of humanity and thus divisive and self-righteous. Indeed, it has been observed that institutional pressures tend to reinforce stage 3 conformity, rather than motivate towards transcending it.[34] Faith development, therefore, may include the struggle to abandon some comfortable, long-held position in order to reach out to a level of greater maturity. In developmental terms, 'disequilibrium' is an important factor in the transition. Hence, the alienating effect of parabolic discourse, especially in dialogue with defended conformist positions, can be part of the process of growth; and every step forward includes the need to become as a *paidion* once more. Such childlike or servant-like re-centring will prevent stage 4 persons from yielding to the insidious temptation to think of themselves more highly than they should. It can also ensure that, at the stage 5 level of human perception, the awareness of paradox does not simply breed despair.

An illuminating commentary on this way of understanding the human response to the Kingdom is provided by a case study of the questioning scribe (Mark 12.28–34): a passage that has received considerable attention in this book. If, as is sometimes suggested,[35] the scribe is simply reflecting the well-rehearsed apologetics of the diaspora Judaism of Mark's day – i.e., that the temple cult has been effectively superseded by obedience to the religious and moral precepts of the Torah – then the scribe's position is no higher than the conformist stage 3 and the debate with Jesus lacks point. Mark's understanding of the situation is quite different. Jesus' commendation of the scribe in 12.34 suggests that, at least in Marcan perspective, the scribe is asking an authentic question and genuinely seeking insight into the divine priorities: a stage 4, 'individuative-reflective' position, exercising critical discrimination. Indeed, his perception may be of an even higher order. Stage 5 perception involves the capacity to discern and accept powerful meanings 'while simultaneously recognizing that they are relative, partial and inevitably distorting apprehensions of transcendental reality'.[36] The scribe may well have come to view the temple cult in this way: it enshrined mighty power, and its performance was a genuine priority for all Israel, yet it must be qualified by the apprehension of the will of God as expressed in the chief commands of the Torah and priority must be given to obeying them. Yet one does not simply abandon the cult and keep the commandments: one observes both as one's response to God, and while accepting the limitations of institutional as well as personal performance, glorifies God in both. 'Truly', said Jesus to the scribe, 'you know the reality of the Kingdom!'

The ultimate goal, towards which all positive development moves, is eschatological. The 'complete man' of Eph. 4.13 represents the goal towards which the Apostle is moving: the mark which he has categorically 'not yet attained'. Even Jesus declined to be called 'good', reserving that term for God alone (Mark 10.18 par.). To be sure, he gave performance to the Kingdom in his ministry, thereby expressing eschatological reality in the human scene; but it is the glorified Christ who is 'seated at the right hand of God'. Impossible as such a goal is for those living within the human life-cycle, the faithful 'press on', and occasionally are 'surprised by joy' as they find themselves giving performance to the Kingdom in their own lives. One might refer here to Reinhold Niebuhr's classic discussion of 'the relevance of an impossible ethical ideal'.[37] The Kingdom, dynamic and invasive as we have seen it to be, interacts with the 'natural' process of development and impels towards transformation, renewal, new growth and flourishing. It brings the vision of a new goal or eschaton, the demonstration of a new quality of existence, and the power of new motivation and resource.

6   PERFORMANCE AND THE ESCHATON

Much has already been said about the relationship of the performance of the Kingdom to eschatology. The Kingdom is eschatological in a whole range of senses: it is final and complete; it is the fulfilment and goal of God's purposes for his creation; it is future and unconditioned. The performance of the Kingdom is the enactment or expression of the Kingdom within the context of the conditioned and historical. It therefore brings eschatology and ethics into mutual interaction. From this there follow some important conclusions.

The first is purely theological. The performance of the Kingdom reflects the dynamic will of God that the Kingdom should be enacted thus in the midst of human history. Henceforth, the focus is not primarily on dreams of future action (though, in various figures, the dimension of longed-for completion is expressed) but on the performance given to the Kingdom by Jesus and the motifs and themes it presents to all who come after him. This is, in theological terms, the decision of God for his creation that reflects and expresses his grace.

The second is christological. Jesus stands at the interface of God's encounter with the world. He is the enactor of the Kingdom in history. Not that the phrase 'bringer of the Kingdom' is particularly appropriate: as has been said above, it is better to speak of the Kingdom bringing Jesus. One should not take a christological standpoint, evolved later in the Church's life, as the criterion for interpreting Jesus' performance of the Kingdom. Rather, his performance of it is the groundwork of Christology. Many features of Jesus' life are unrelated to this performance: the fact that he was male and Jewish, for example, does not preclude females and Gentiles from performing the Kingdom. Such particularities occur simply because the Kingdom is brought to performance by a particular person in a particular, socio-historical context.

The third is motivational. The 'natural' process of human development, as we have just seen, is prone to the prisonhouse of convention or egotism unless it is surprised by grace; and, in its later stages particularly, is liable to lapse into despair and disintegration. Engagement with the Kingdom not only brings 'new birth' – the Johannine term for 'becoming as a child' – but a motivation and dynamic which takes one through the various levels of development, enabling one to overcome or obviate the dangers which each level brings. Hence one 'grows in grace', specifically through the performance of the Kingdom.

The fourth is teleological: it has to do with goal. The fullness towards which one grows is eschatological: 'the measure of the stature of the fulness of Christ' (Eph. 4.13). The Christ exalted through suffering embodies the eschatological goal. For all human beings, the goal is future, and no 'realized eschatology' can be permitted to eliminate this future element, for with it would depart the teleological perspective essential to life within the Kingdom (cf. Matt. 5.48).

The fifth is historical and political. The performance of the Kingdom takes place not only in time and place but also within given cultural and societal structures. Without the qualifications which a transcendent perspective brings, there is always a tendency for such structures and conventions to make absolute claims for themselves. In such a situation, the Kingdom poses fundamental and ultimately undermining questions. It is no accident that the Gospel writers were keenly aware of the likelihood of persecution, even though they clearly distanced themselves from the forces of overt rebellion. Nor is it an accident that totalitarian powers today look with much suspicion on religious traditions which assert a transcendental perspective. Of course, this is equally true of democratic societies which select for themselves materialistic goals and the pursuit of power as primary aims.

The sixth and last conclusion concerns ministry and community. The performance of the Kingdom in the ministry of Jesus created a special kind of community, geared to ministry and service. It is this kind of community that is peculiarly 'eschatological' – shot through with ultimate concern, and enacting God's Kingdom on earth. At its heart is a sharing, self-giving ministry, symbolized and expressed in the Lord's Supper. It may or may not precisely coincide today with the institutional Church; but equally it cannot without qualification be ascribed to the 'small group' situation, for small groups may be of many types: in their intensity, they can frequently reinforce a stage 3 position rather than actively foster further growth and development. Where the community bears the marks of the self-giving of Jesus, there is the context for renewal, mission and nurture. There, however inceptively, the Kingdom is given performance and reality in the midst of the world.

NOTES

1 Linnemann (1966), pp. 30–3.
2 'Performative utterance' is, like 'language event', also an inheritance from the 1960s, at least in theology. While a language event is conceived of from the hearer's point of view, as what speech compels from him, a performative utterance is a statement by a person which brings into being what it speaks of. Evidently, the designation 'performative utterance' is also existentially grounded (cf. Anthony C. Thiselton [1980], pp. 336–7). Speech can only bring into being in the sense that a possibility exists; apart from the understanding that what *might* be actually exists in human terms, nothing is performed by speech except a manipulation of language. (Precisely that perspective on 'performatives' has recently been argued, cf. John R. Searle [1970], and it accords in certain basic features with the initial approach of John L. Austin [1961].) 'Performance' permits statements to be exhibitions of language, without assuming that they necessarily invoke realities.

The relationship between speech and reality is a problematic one. The influence of Ludwig Wittgenstein within linguistics has tended to result in an understanding of language, not as the field of human being, but as serious human play which follows its own rules (cf. Thiselton [1980], pp. 357–85). Structuralist linguistics, particularly as developed by Noam Chomsky, referred the game of language to inherently human facilities, so that speaking was seen as the realization of linguistic, rather than existential, possibilities (Chomsky, 1972). Chomsky's analysis pushed language and reality further apart, and precisely that has been the tendency of linguistic philosophy overall. Before language was conceived of existentially, it was widely seen as a denotative reference to what could be perceived. Existentially understood, language refers to human possibility, rather than to what tangibly is. As understood structurally, language is, in effect, self-referential: the game is played for its own sake.

Even Chomsky's reference to an inherently human facility for language has been attacked as excessively metaphysical. The insistence is increasingly voiced that language is acquired, rather than evolved, by individual human beings; linguistic competence is not given inherently with the fact of being human, but is learned within particular social settings (Bruce L. Derwing, 1973). From that perspective, language is a practically autonomous phenomenon, and to ask after its relationship to reality is a matter merely of the psychology of learning. To posit any closer reference is a metaphysical claim, rather than a linguistic or philosophical argument. The most rudimentary acquaintance with modern approaches to linguistics leaves little room for confident assertions about what language, not to speak of parabolic language, refers to (if anything). The philosophy of language can, and has, contributed to literary study, including the literary study of the New Testament. But linguistic philosophy has not produced a sufficiently coherent account of how words convey meaning to enable us to employ it directly as a description of how the preaching of the Kingdom functions. 'Performance', then, refers simply to an instance of speaking, and implies no claim that such speaking determines or describes what is true.

3   Crossan (1983), pp. 37–40. Crossan distinguishes between *ipsissima structura* and *ipsissima verba* in order to contrast sense and wording.
4   See Jacob Neusner (1985).
5   See Birger Gerhardsson (1979).
6   Crossan, op. cit., pp. 39–40.
7   ibid., p. 41.
8   ibid., pp. 50–1, 54.
9   Crossan's basic point, derived from Bultmann and Manson (pp. 50–1), is sound: the attempt to construe Jesus' saying as antithetical to early Jewish formulations is ill-founded. The negative formulation in some Christian sources, notably Thomas 6b and *Didache* 1.2b (cf. C. Taylor [1886], pp. 8–11, 18–23), underscores that point.
10 Crossan seems to have had this aphorism in mind early on in his volume, because he specifies the shift 'from positive to negative, or vice versa' as the meaning of 'conversion' (p. 39). In fact, conversion may be said to characterize several grammatical and syntactical shifts. For example, tense may be changed, third person and second person forms might be used to the same effect, and pronouns or nouns can be varied, all without altering meaning substantially. Variation of tense is evident in the saying, variously attributed to Jesus, in respect of des-

troying the temple (Matt. 26.61/Mark 14.58; cf. John 2.19 for another, but comparable, conversion); the shift between second and third persons is instanced by the beatitudes (Matt. 5.3–11/Luke 6.20b–22); pronominal variations appear within the Marcan presentation of the command to listen attentively (Mark 4.9, 23). Such grammatical conversions do not account exhaustively for the differences among these sayings, and other shifts of the same nature might be adduced, but those mentioned do illustrate that a saying can be conveyed by differing grammatical modes.

11   Crossan (1983), pp. 57–66.

12   ibid., pp. 37–66.

13   Bernard Brandon Scott (1985) has rightly criticized Crossan at precisely this point: the aphoristic core, which is the end of study, is nothing more than 'a system of possibilities' (p. 20). We might put the same criticism differently by observing that Crossan sacrifices texts to the linguistic structures texts are alleged to articulate. His predilection for *ipsissima structura* begs the linguistic issues involved in structuralism, which have already been mentioned, and makes the object of study unclear.

14   cf. Scott (1981), p. 99.

15   cf. Fries (1982), pp. 33–45. His system is a considerable adjustment of Kant's, in which the moral imperative is more autonomously conveyed by practical reason.

16   Ritschl (1902), pp. 30–1.

17   Weiss (1900), p. v; cf. Chilton, *Kingdom* (1984).

18   cf. Mathews (1897), pp. 198–230; Rauschenbusch (1917), pp. 131–45.

19   cf. McCown (1929), pp. 321–8.

20   cf. Edwin R. Yamauchi (1973), pp. 73–9.

21   cf. Otto (1934), p. 80; Dodd (1936), p. 45 n.1.

22   cf. Freire (1972), pp. 45–59.

23   Jeremias (1954), pp. 89–158.

24   cf. Nineham (1976).

25   Lit. 'setting in the life of Jesus', a prime concern of the form-critical method.

26   cf. Weiss (1900); Perrin (1976).

27   cf. McLuhan (1962).

28   cf. Holub (1984).

29   cf. Detweiler, *Semeia* 31.

30   cf. Dunn (1986).

31   cf. Fairweather and McDonald (1984), pp. 238–43.

32   Fowler (1981), p. 4. Fowler's stages of faith may be summarized as follows:
pre-stage: 'undifferentiated' faith (not unlike Erikson's 'basic trust'): characterizes children in their first two years.
stage 1: 'intuitive-projective' faith ('intuitive' refers to the fact that emotional interests tend to be the focus of thinking; 'projective' indicates the tendency to project the characteristics of parents on to

the screen of faith): characterizes children of about two to six years.

stage 2: 'mythic literal' faith ('mythic' refers to story: people at this stage live out their story but do not stand back to reflect on it): characterizes children of about seven to twelve years but, as Fowler notes, many adults seem content to live at this level.

stage 3: 'synthetic conventional' faith – the conformist, inter-personal stage characteristic of adolescence: perhaps the majority of adults live at this level.

stage 4: 'individuative-reflective' faith – when one develops a more independent awareness of one's faith, one's relationships and one's world, and takes personal responsibility for one's decisions.

stage 5: 'conjunctive' faith – recognizing the paradoxes of faith and life, but having sufficient maturity to hold together conflicting elements of reality: not usually found before mid-life.

stage 6: 'universalizing' faith – in which the particularity of one's existence is constantly informed by the universal: the level of the saints!

33   Furushima (1985).

34   cf. Hull (1985), p. 189f.

35   cf. Fuller (1978), p. 47, where he follows Bornkamm in ascribing 'the preference of the moral law over the sacrificial cult' to 'a Hellenistic-Jewish rather than a rabbinic understanding of the law'. Paul's readiness to appeal to the principle of the temple tax illustrates the evocative power of the temple symbol in the Hellenistic-Jewish world, at least in Paul's time.

36   Fowler (1981), p. 198.

37   Niebuhr (1936), pp. 113–45.

Bibliography

Allison, D. C., *The End of the Ages has Come*. Philadelphia, Fortress, 1985.

Auerbach, E., *Mimesis*. New York, Doubleday, 1957.

Aune, D. E., *Prophecy in Early Christianity and the Ancient Mediterranean World*. Grand Rapids, Eerdmans, 1983.

Austin, J. L., (ed. J. O. Urmson, G. J. Warnock), *Philosophical Papers*. Oxford, Clarendon, 1961.

Bald, H., 'Eschatologische oder theozentrische Ethik? Anmerkungen zum Problem einer Verhältnisbestimmung von Eschatologie und Ethik in der Verkündigung Jesu', *Verkündigung und Forschung* 24 (1979), pp. 35–52; an English tr. is present in the *The Kingdom of God in the Teaching of Jesus* (see under Chilton), pp. 133–53.

Baldensperger, W., *Das Selbtbewusstsein Jesu im Lichte der messianischen Hoffnungen seiner Zeit*. Strasburg, Heitz, 1888.

Bammel, E., 'The revolution theory from Reimarus to Brandon', *Jesus and the Politics of his Day*, (ed. E. Bammel and C. F. D. Moule) (Cambridge, Cambridge University Press, 1984), pp. 11–68.

——, 'The Poor and the Zealots', *Jesus and the Politics of his Day*, pp. 109–28.

——, 'The Trial Before Pilate', *Jesus and the Politics of his Day*, pp. 415–51.

Barrett, C. K., 'Shaliaḥ and Apostle', *Donum Gentilicium. New Testament Studies in Honour of David Daube* (ed. E. Bammel, C. K. Barrett, W. D. Davies) (Oxford, Clarendon, 1978), pp. 88–102.

Becker, Joachim, (E. tr. D. E. Green), *Messianic Expectations in the Old Testament*. Philadelphia, Fortress, 1980.

Becker, Jürgen, *Untersuchungen zur Entstehungsgeschichte der Testamente der Zwölf Patriarchen*. Leiden, Brill, 1970.

Best, E., *Following Jesus. Discipleship in the Gospel of Mark*. Sheffield, JSOT, 1981.

Black, M., 'The Marcan Parable of the Child in the Midst', *Expository Times* 59 (1947-8), pp. 14-16.

Bornkamm, G., 'Das Doppelgebot der Liebe', *Neutestamentliche Studien für Rudolf Bultmann*: Biehefte zur Zeitschrift für die neutestamentlichen Wissenschaft 21. Berlin, Töpelmann, 1957.

Borsch, F. H., *The Son of Man in Myth and History*. London, SCM, 1967.

Brandon, S. G. F., *Jesus and the Zealots*. Manchester, Manchester University Press, 1967.

Braun, H., *Jesus*. Stuttgart, Kreuz, 1969.

Breech, E., 'Kingdom of God and the Parables of Jesus', *Semeia* 12 (1978), pp. 14-40.

Bright, J., *A History of Israel*. London, SCM, 1962.

Buber, M., *Kingdom of God*. London, Allen & Unwin, 1967.

Bultmann, R., *Die Erforschung der synoptischen Evangelien*: Aus der Welt der Religion. Berlin, Töpelmann, 1961.

——, 'Jesus Christus und die Mythologie', *Glauben und Verstehen* 4 (Mohr, Tübingen, 1965), pp. 141-89, which appeared earlier as *Jesus Christ and Mythology* (New York, Scribner, 1958).

——, *Theologie des Neuen Testaments*. Tübingen, Mohr, 1977.

Burchard, C., 'The Theme of the Sermon on the Mount', *Essays on the Love Commandment* (ed. L. Schottroff et al.) (Philadelphia, Fortress, 1978), pp. 57-91.

Cameron, P. S., *Violence and the Kingdom. The Interpretation of Matthew 11:12*. Frankfurt am Main, Lang, 1984.

Cardenal, E., (E. tr. D. D. Walsh), *Love in Practice. The Gospel in Solentiname*. London, Search Press, 1977.

Catchpole, D. R., 'The "Triumphal Entry"', *Jesus and the Politics of his Day* (see under Bammel), pp. 319-34.

Chilton, B. D., *A Galilean Rabbi and his Bible. Jesus' Use of the Interpreted Scripture of his Time*: Good News Studies 8. Wilmington, Glazier, 1984, publ. with the subtitle *Jesus' own interpretation of Isaiah* by SPCK, London, 1984.

——, *God in Strength. Jesus' Announcement of the Kingdom*: Studien zum Neuen Testament und seiner Umwelt. Friestadt, Plöchl, 1979.

——, 'The Glory of Israel. The Theology and Provenience of the Isaiah Targum', *Journal for the Study of the Old Testament* 23 (1982).

——, *The Isaiah Targum: Translation, Introduction, Apparatus, and Notes*: The Aramaic Bible. Wilmington, Glazier, 1987.

——, ed., *The Kingdom of God in the Teaching of Jesus*: Issues in Religion and Theology. London, SPCK, and Philadelphia, Fortress, 1984.

Chomsky, N., *Language and Mind*. New York, Harcourt Brace Jovanovich, 1972.

Clarke, W. K. L., *New Testament Problems*. London, SPCK, 1929.

Clements, R. E., *Prophecy and Tradition*. Oxford, Blackwell, 1975.

Colpe, C., '*Ho huios tou anthrôpou*', *Theological Dictionary of the New Testament* 8 (1972; for further details, see under Jeremias), pp. 400–77.

Conzelmann, H., *Grundriss der Theologie des Neuen Testaments*. Munich, Kaiser, 1967.

——, (E. tr. G. Buswell), *The Theology of Saint Luke*. London, Faber & Faber, 1960.

Cranfield, C. E. B., *The Gospel according to Saint Mark*. Cambridge, Cambridge University Press, 1959.

Crossan, J. D., *The Dark Interval. Towards a Theology of Story*. Niles, Argus, 1975.

——, *In Fragments. The Aphorisms of Jesus*. New York, Harper & Row, 1983.

——, 'Kingdom and Children: a Study in the Aphoristic Tradition', *Semeia* 29 (1983), pp. 75–95.

——, *In Parables. The Challenge of the Historical Jesus*. New York, Harper & Row, 1973.

Dalman, G. H., (E. tr. D. M. McKay), *The Words of Jesus considered in the light of post-biblical Jewish writings and the Aramaic language*. Edinburgh, T. & T. Clark, 1902.

de Jonge, M., 'The Use of the Word "Anointed" in the Time of Jesus', *Novum Testamentum* 8 (1966), pp. 132–48.

Derrida, J., *Of Grammatology*. Baltimore, Johns Hopkins, 1980.

Derwing, B. L., *Transformational Grammar as a Theory of Language Acquisition. A Study in the Empirical, Conceptual, and Methodological Foundations of Contemporary Linguistics*. Cambridge, Cambridge University Press, 1973.

Detweiler, R., 'Reader Response Approaches to Biblical and Sacred Texts', *Semeia* 31 (1985).

Di Lella, A. A., and Hartman, L. F., *The Book of Daniel*: Anchor Bible. Garden City, Doubleday, 1978.

Dillmann, R., *Das Eigentliche der Ethik Jesu. Ein exegetischen Beitrag zur moraltheologischen Diskussion um das Proprium einer christlichen Ethik*. Tübingen Theologische Studien 23, Mainz, Matthias-Grünewald, 1984.

Dodd, C. H., *The Parables of the Kingdom*. London, Nisbet, 1936.

——, *Gospel and Law*. Cambridge, Cambridge University Press, 1957.

Dunn, J. D. G., *Jesus and the Spirit*. London, SCM, 1975.

——, ed., *The Kingdom of God in North East England Today*. London, SCM, 1986.

Dupont, J., *Les Beatitudes* III. Paris, Gabalda, 1973.

Eisler, R., *The Messiah Jesus and John the Baptist*. London, Methuen, 1931.

Etheridge, J. W., *The Targums of Onkelos and Jonathan ben Uzziel*. New York, Ktav, 1968, from the edn of 1862.

Fairweather, I. C. M., and McDonald, J. I. H., *The Quest for Christian Ethics*. Edinburgh, Handsel, 1984.

Flender, H., (E. tr. R. H. Fuller and I. Fuller), *St Luke, Theologian of Redemptive History*. London, SPCK, 1967.

Fletcher, J., *Situation Ethics. The New Morality*. London, SCM, 1966.

Flusser, D., *Die rabbinische Gleichnisse und der Gleichniserzähler Jesus 1. Teil: Das Wesen der Gleichnisse*: Judaica et Christiana. Las Vegas, Lang, 1981.

Forrester, D. B., McDonald, J. I. H., Tellini, G., *Encounter with God*. Edinburgh, T. & T. Clark, 1983.

Fowler, J. W., *Stages of Faith. The Psychology of Human Development and the Quest for Meaning*. San Francisco, Harper & Row, 1981.

Freedman, H., *Shabbath*: The Babylonian Talmud (ed. I. Epstein). London, Soncino, 1938; also in the diglot edition of 1972.

Freire, P., *Pedagogy of the Oppressed*. London, Sheed & Ward, 1972.

Fries, J. F. (ed. D. Z. Phillips, E. tr. D. Walford), *Dialogues on Morality and Religion* (selections from *Julius und Evagoras* [Heidelberg, Winter, 1822]). Totowa, Barnes & Noble, and Oxford, Basil Blackwell, 1982.

Fuller, R. H., 'The Double Commandment of Love: A Test Case for the Criteria of Authenticity', *Essays on the Love Commandment* (see under Burchard), pp. 41–56.

Furnish, V. P., *The Love Command in the New Testament*. London, SCM, 1973.

Furushima, R., 'Faith Development in a Cross Cultural Perspective', *Religious Education* 80 (1985), pp. 414–20.

Gaster, T. H., *The Dead Sea Scriptures in English. Translation with Introduction and Notes*. Garden City, Doubleday, 1976.

Gereboff, J., *Rabbi Tarfon. The Tradition, the Man, and Early Judaism*. Brown University Judaic Studies 7. Missoula, Scholars, 1979.

Gerhardsson, B., *The Ethos of the Bible*. London, Darton, Longman & Todd, 1982.

——, *The Origins of the Gospel Traditions*. Philadelphia, Fortress, 1979.

Gibson, J. C. L., *Genesis* I. Edinburgh, St Andrew Press, and Philadelphia, Westminster, 1981.

Gray, J., *The Biblical Doctrine of the Reign of God*. Edinburgh, T. & T. Clark, 1979.

Hartman, A. A. (see under Di Lella).

Hengel, M., (E. tr. J. Greig), *The Charismatic Leader and his Followers*. Edinburgh, T. & T. Clark, 1981.

——, (E. tr. W. Classen), *Was Jesus a Revolutionist?* Philadelphia, Facet, 1971.

Higger, M., *Treatise Semaḥoth*. New York, Bloch, 1931.

Higgins, A. J. B., *The Son of Man in the Teaching of Jesus*. Cambridge, Cambridge University Press, 1980.

Holub, R., *Reception Theory. A Critical Introduction*. London, Methuen, 1984.

Hooker, M. D., *The Message of Mark*. London, Epworth, 1983.

Hull, J. M., *What Prevents Christian Adults from Learning?* London, SCM, 1985.

Israelstram, J., *Aboth*: The Babylonian Talmud (ed. I. Epstein). London, Soncino, 1935.

Jeremias, J., (E. tr. D. Cairns), *Infant Baptism in the First Four Centuries*. London, SCM, 1960.

——, (E. tr. F. H. Cave and C. H. Cave), *Jerusalem in the Time of Jesus*. London, SCM, 1969.

——, (E. tr. S. H. Hooke), *The Parables of Jesus*. London, SCM, 1976; the German editions of Zwingli Verlag (Zürich 1947), and Vandenhoeck & Ruprecht (Göttingen 1977), were also consulted.

——, '*Poimēn ktl.*', *Theological Dictionary of the New Testament* 6 (ed. G. Friedrich, G. W. Bromiley) (Grand Rapids, Eerdmans, 1979), pp. 485–502.

Johnson, A. R., *Sacral Kingship in Ancient Israel*. Cardiff, University of Wales Press, 1967.

Jung, C. G., (ed. H. Read, M. Fordham, and G. Adler), *The Collected Works of C. G. Jung*: Bollingen Series. New York, Pantheon, 1968.

Kee, H. C., '"Becoming a Child" in the Gospel of Thomas', *Journal of Biblical Literature* 82 (1963), pp. 307–14.

Kelber, W. H., 'Mark and Oral Tradition', *Semeia* 16 (1980), pp. 7–55.

——, *The Oral and Written Gospel. The Hermeneutics of Speaking and Writing in the Synoptic Tradition, Mark, Paul, and Q*. Philadelphia, Fortress, 1983.

——, ed., *The Passion in Mark. Studies on Mark 14–16*. Philadelphia, Fortress, 1976.

Kermode, J. F., *The Genesis of Secrecy. On the Interpretation of Narrative*. Cambridge, Mass., Harvard University Press, 1979.

Krause, G., ed., *Die Kinder im Evangelium*, Stuttgart, Klotz, 1973.

Legasse, S., 'L'Enfant dans l'Évangile', *La Vie Spirituelle* 570 (1970), pp. 409–21.

——, *Jésus et l'Enfant*. Paris, Gabalda, 1969.

Lehmann, P. L., *Ethics in a Christian Context*. New York, Harper & Row, 1976.

Leivestad, R., 'Der apokalypstische Menschensohn: ein theologisches Phantom', *Annual of the Swedish Theological Institute* 6 (1968), pp. 49–105.

——, 'Exit the Apocalyptic Son of Man', *New Testament Studies* 18 (1971–2), pp. 243–67.

Lindars, B., *Jesus, Son of Man*. London, SPCK, 1983.

——, 'John and the Synoptic Gospels: A Test Case', *New Testament Studies* 27 (1981), pp. 287–94.

Linnemann, E. (E. tr. J. Sturdy), *Jesus of the Parables: Introduction and Exposition*. New York, Harper & Row, 1966, from the German edn of 1964 (Göttingen, Vandenhoeck & Ruprecht).

Lührmann, D., 'Liebet eure Feinde (Lk. 6.27–36/Mt. 5.38–48)', *Zeitschrift für Theologie und Kirche* 69 (1972), pp. 412–38.

McCown, C. C., *The Genesis of the Social Gospel. The Meaning of the Ideals of Jesus in the Light of Their Antecedents*. New York, Knopf, 1929.

McDonald, J. I. H., *Kerygma and Didache*. Cambridge, Cambridge University Press, 1980.

——, 'Receiving and Entering the Kingdom: A Study of Mark 10.15', *Studia Evangelica* VI (1973), pp. 328–32.

—— (see under Fairweather and Forrester).

Mackey, J. P., *Jesus. The Man and the Myth*. London, SCM, 1979.

McLuhan, M., *The Gutenberg Galaxy*. London, Routledge & Keagan Paul, 1962.

McNamara, M., *Targum and Testament. Aramaic Paraphrases of the Hebrew Bible: A New Light on the New Testament*. Shannon, Irish University Press, 1972.

Manson, T. W., *Ethics and the Gospel*. London, SCM, 1960.

——, *The Teaching of Jesus*. Cambridge, Cambridge University Press, 1935.

Martelet, G., (E. tr. R. Hague), *The Risen Christ and the Eucharistic World*. London, Collins, 1976.

Mathews, S., *The Social Teaching of Jesus. An Essay in Christian Sociology*. New York, Macmillan, 1897.

Mealand, D. L., *Poverty and Expectation in the Gospels*. London, SPCK, 1980.

Meecham, H. G., *The Oldest Version of the Bible*. London, Holborn, 1932.

Merklein, H., *Die Gottesherrschaft als Handlungsprinzip. Untersuchung zur Ethik Jesu*: Forschung zur Bibel. Wurzburg, Echter Verlag, 1978.

Meyer, B. F., *The Aims of Jesus*. London, SCM, 1979.

Miller, D. L., *Christs: Meditations on Archetypal Images in Christian Theology*. New York, Seabury, 1981.

Minear, P.S., *Commands of Christ*. Edinburgh, St Andrew Press, 1972.

Mussner, F., 'Der nicht erkannte Kairos (Matth. 11.16–19, Luk. 7.31–35)', *Biblica* 40 (1959), pp. 599–612.

Neusner, J., *The Peripatetic Saying. The Problem of the Thrice-Told Tale in Talmudic Literature*. Brown Judaic Studies 89. Chico, Scholars Press, 1985.

Niebuhr, R., *An Interpretation of Christian Ethics*. London, SCM, 1936.

Nineham, D., *The Use and Abuse of the Bible*. London, SPCK, 1976.

Oepke, A., '*Pais, ktl.*', *Theological Dictionary of the New Testament* 5 (1978, for further details, see under Jeremias), pp. 636–54.

Oldfather, W. A., *Epictetus. The Discourses as Reported by Arrian, The Manual, and Fragments*. Loeb Classical Library. London, Heinemann, 1926.

O'Neill, J. C., *Messiah. Six Lectures on the Ministry of Jesus*. Cambridge, Cochrane, 1980.

Otto, R., (E. tr. J. W. Harvey), *The Idea of the Holy* (from the German edn of 1917). London, Oxford University Press, 1928.

——, (E. tr. F. V. Filson and B. L. Woolf), *The Kingdom of God and the Son of Man* (from the German edn of 1934). London, Lutterworth, 1938.

——, (E. tr. E. B. Dicker), *The Philosophy of Religion based on Kant and Fries* (from the German edn of 1909). London, Williams & Norgate, 1931.

Pedersen, J., *Israel, its Life and Culture*. London, Cumberlege, 1926.

Perrin, N., *Jesus and the Language of the Kingdom*. London, SCM, 1976.

——, *The New Testament. An Introduction*. New York, Harcourt Brace Jovanovich, 1974.

——, *Rediscovering the Teaching of Jesus*. London, SCM, 1967.

Pettit, P., *The Concept of Structuralism: A Critical Analysis*. Berkeley, University of California Press, 1975.

Petuchowski, J. J., 'Jewish Prayer Texts of the Rabbinic Period', *The Lord's Prayer and Jewish Liturgy* (ed. J. J. Petuchowski and M. Brocke) (London, Burns & Oates, 1968), pp. 21–44.

Piper, J., 'Love Your Enemies'. Cambridge, Cambridge University Press, 1979.

Rauschenbusch, W., The Righteousness of the Kingdom (ed. M. L. Stackhouse). New York, Abingdon, 1968.

——, A Theology for the Social Gospel. New York, Macmillan, 1917.

Rawlinson, A. E. J., St Mark. London, Methuen, 1925.

Ritschl, A. B., (E. tr. H. R. Mackintosh and A. B. Macauly), The Christian Doctrine of Justification and Reconciliation (from the German edition of 1888). Edinburgh, T. & T. Clark, 1902.

Robbins, V. K., 'Pronouncement Stories and Jesus' Blessing of the Children: a rhetorical approach', Semeia 29 (1983), pp. 43–74.

Sanders, E. P., Paul and Palestinian Judaism. A Comparison of Patterns of Religion. London, SCM, and Philadelphia, Fortress, 1977.

——, Jesus and Judaism. London, SCM, and Philadelphia, Fortress, 1985.

Sauer, J., 'Der ursprüngliche "Sitz im Lebem" von Mk. 10. 13–16', Zeitschrift für die neutestamentliche Wissenschaft 72 (1981), pp. 27–50.

Schelling, F. A., 'What Means the Saying about Receiving the Kingdom of God as a Little Child?', Expository Times 77 (1966), pp. 56–8.

Schillebeeckx, E. C., (E. tr. H. Hoskins), Jesus. An Experiment in Christology. London, Collins, 1979.

Schneider, G., 'The Political Charge against Jesus (Luke 23.2)', Jesus and the Politics of his Day (see under Bammel), pp. 403–14.

Schottroff, L., 'The Ethics of Liberation – The Liberation of Ethics', Concilium 172 (1984), pp. 67–73.

——, 'Non-Violence and the Love of One's Enemies', Essays on the Love Commandment (see under Burchard), pp. 9–39.

Schürmann, H., Gottes Reich – Jesu Geschick. Jesu ureigner Tod im Lichte seiner Basilei-Verkündigung. Freiburg, Herder, 1983.

Scott, B. B., Jesus, Symbol-maker for the Kingdom. Philadelphia, Fortress, 1981.

——, 'Picking up the Pieces', Forum 1 (1985), pp. 15–21.

Searle, J. R., Speech Acts. An Essay in the Philosophy of Language. Cambridge, Cambridge University Press, 1970.

Schweitzer, A., (E. tr. W. Montgomery), The Quest of the Historical Jesus. New York, Macmillan, 1922, 1954, from Geschichte der Leben-Jesu-Forschung (Mohr, Tübingen, 1913).

Scroggs, R., 'The New Testament and Ethics: How do We Get from There to Here?', Perspectives on the New Testament. Essays in Honor of Frank Stagg (ed. C. H. Talbert). Macon, Mercer University Press, 1985.

Seung, T. K., *Structuralism and Hermeneutics*. New York, Columbia University Press, 1982.

Silberman, L. H., 'Schoolboys and Storytellers: Some Comments on Aphorisms and *Chriae*', *Semeia* 29 (1983), pp. 109–15.

Slingerland, H. D., *The Testaments of the Twelve Patriarchs. A Critical History of Research*: Society of Biblical Literature Monograph Series 21. Missoula, Scholars, 1977.

Smart, J. D., *The Past, Present and Future of Biblical Theology*. Philadelphia, Westminster, 1979.

Sperber, A., *The Bible in Aramaic* (III) *The Latter Prophets*. Leiden, Brill, 1962.

Spohn, W. G., *What Are They Saying About Scripture and Ethics?* New York, Paulist, 1984.

Stauffer, E., *Die Botschaft Jesu, Damals und Heute*. Dalp-Taschenbücher 33. Bern, Franche, 1959.

Stein, R. H., 'The "Criteria" for Authenticity', *Gospel Perspectives* I (ed. R. T. France and D. Wenham) (Sheffield, JSOT, 1983), pp. 225–63.

Stendahl, K., 'Matthew', *Peake's Commentary on the Bible* (ed M. Black and H. H. Rowley) (London, Nelson, 1962), pp. 769–98.

Stroup, G. W., *The Promise of Narrative Theology*. Atlanta, Knox, 1981, and London, SCM, 1984.

Sweet, J. P. M., 'The Zealots and Jesus', *Jesus and the Politics of his Day* (see under Bammel), pp. 1–9.

Tannehill, R. C., 'The Gospel of Mark as Narrative Christology', *Semeia* 16 (1980), pp. 578–95.

Taylor, C., *The Teaching of the Twleve Apostles with Illustrations from the Talmud*. Cambridge, Deighton Bell, 1886.

Telford, W. R., *The Barren Temple and the Withered Tree*. Sheffield, JSOT, 1980.

Tellini, G. (see under Forrester).

TeSelle, S. McFague, *Speaking in Parables. A Study in Metaphor and Theology*. Philadelphia, Fortress, 1975.

Thiselton, A. C., *The Two Horizons. New Testament Hermeneutics and Philosophical Description with Special Reference to Heidegger, Bultmann, Gadamer, and Wittgenstein*. Grand Rapids, Eerdmans, 1980.

Tracy, D., *Blessed Rage for Order. The New Pluralism in Theology*. New York, Seabury, 1978.

Tugwell, S., *Reflections on the Beatitudes*. London, Darton, Longman and Todd, 1980.

Vermes, G., *The Dead Sea Scrolls in English*. Harmondsworth, Penguin, 1962.

——, *The Gospel of Jesus the Jew*. Newcastle, University of Newcastle, 1981.

——, *Jesus the Jew. A Historian's Reading of the Gospels*. London, Collins, 1973; Fontana, 1976.

Via, D. O., *The Ethics of Mark's Gospel in the Middle of Time*. Philadelphia, Fortress, 1985.

——, *The Parables: Their Literary and Existential Dimension*. Philadelphia, Fortress, 1967.

Wainwright, G., *Eucharist and Eschatology*. London, Epworth, 1978.

Weber, H. R., *Jesus and the Children*. Geneva, World Council of Churches, 1979.

Weiss, J., *Die Predigt Jesu vom Reiche Gottes*. Göttingen, Vandenhoeck & Ruprecht, 1892, of which the second edn appeared in 1900 (reprinted in 1964).

——, (E. tr. R. H. Hiers and D. L. Holland), *Jesus' Proclamation of the Kingdom of God*. Philadelphia, Fortress, 1971.

Whitelam, K., *The Just King*. Sheffield, JSOT, 1979.

Williams, J. G., *Gospel against Parable. Mark's Language of Mystery*. Sheffield, Almond, 1985.

Wink, W., *John the Baptist in Gospel Tradition*. Cambridge, Cambridge University Press, 1968.

Wright, G. E., *God Who Acts: Biblical Theology as Recital*. London, SCM, 1952.

——, *The Old Testament and Theology*. New York, Harper & Row, 1972.

Yamauchi, Edwin R., *Pre-Christian Gnosticism. A Survey of the Proposed Evidences*. London, Tyndale, 1973.

Yoder, J., *The Politics of Jesus*. Grand Rapids, Eerdmans, 1972.

Index of Biblical References

Index of Names and Subjects